# DEVELOPING A PERSONAL RELATIONSHIP WITH GOD: THE ONE WHO CREATED THE UNIVERSE.

A PERSONAL REFLECTION FROM
MY SPIRITUAL ODYSSEY
RICHARD ELLIOTT

ARCHWAY
PUBLISHING

Archway Publishing books may be ordered through booksellers or by contacting:

Archway Publishing
1663 Liberty Drive
Bloomington, IN 47403
www.archwaypublishing.com
844-669-3957

ISBN: 978-1-6657-5111-7 (sc)
ISBN: 978-1-6657-5217-6 (hc)
ISBN: 978-1-6657-5110-0 (e)

Library of Congress Control Number: 2023919151

Print information available on the last page.

Archway Publishing rev. date: 10/26/2023

# CONTENTS

# ABOUT THE AUTHOR

The journey continues, but the destination remains predictably uncertain for Richard Elliott, a consummate seeker who never hesitates to explore new faith dimensions. Rarely content with the spiritual staus quo, but regularly focused on digging deeper, he enjoys inviting others to venture into previously uncharted territory. Delightfully honest, downright frank and always well-intentioned are but a few ways I would describe my friend and brother in Christ. A man of deep convictions and a mature but ever inquiring faith, he never tires in his efforts to grow spiritually, be present to those in need and make a meaningful difference in the lives of others, whether that be family, friends or a stranger on the street. Gifted with a knack for accepting perspectives that may differ from his, he consistently displays a refreshing openness that often brings reconciliation, healing and peace. A seed sower whose goal is always to produce a meaningfull harvest, it's fascinating to watch this perpetual planter at work. May those who read Richard's most recent work, which is rooted firmly in the fertile soil of new perspectives, discover a rich assortment of gems worth pondering and helpful insights deserving additional contemplation. My guess is this will not be his last book. I continue to treasure the rather unique relationship I am privileged to share with a special saint, Richard Elliott.     Eric Wogan, retired ELC Pastor

I have worshipped, served in Christian outreach, and been

friends in life and Christ with Richard since he, his wife Carol and others help bring me back to active faith formation a decade ago. Richard is an authentic disciple and the ultimate seeker. The sincerity and passion of his commitment to keeping God, Christ and the Spirit at the center of his life, and his willingness to help others like me do the same, are human values that are far too rare in this age in which we live.   Steve Blackledge

Throughout history, man has tried to understand how to get close to God. In most cases, he has followed a one-sided dogmatic theory from religious organizations. Richard Elliott gives us the information to find out for ourselves. He shows us the path to discovery Gods on the personal level. I firmly believe this is a groundbreaking book.   Paul Gonzalez, radio and TV broadcaster

# DEDICATION

I dedicate "Developing a Personal Relationship with God: The One Who Created the Universe. A Personal Reflection From My Spiritual Odyssey" to the following individuals who have inspired me to change my wayward ways and become a true Christian:

1.  My wife, Carol
2.  My two daughters, Susan and Elizabeth
3.  Pastor Eric Wogen

I am grateful to the Lord for their support, guidance, and for standing by me a s I slowly change my ways and devote my life to Christ.

# ACKNOWLEDGEMENTS

I would like to express my gratitude to my friends and neighbors at Sunnyside Village who encouraged me to complete this project. I am especially thankful to Tom Coffing, Greg Envey, Terry Envey, Ann Giel, Julie Howell, and Beth Miller for their valuable feedback and unwavering support.

I would also like to extend a special acknowledgment to Eric Wogen for his spiritual and editorial guidance throughout this project. Eric's constant encouragement and support were instrumental in enabling me to complete my book, DEVELOPING A PERSONAL RELATIONSHIP WITH GOD THE ONE WHO CREATED THE UNIVERSE. A Personal Reflection From My Spiritual Odyssey.

It is my sincere hope and prayer that all who read this book will be inspired to develop a personal relationship with their God and strengthen their spirituality to recognize God in all aspects of life.

# PREFACE

The God of your understanding is that:
the God of your understanding.
What you need is the God
just beyond your understanding.

Rami Shapiro

The appendices in this book will appear at the end of each chapter they are referred to. They are placed there for the readers' convenience to be able to immediately read the additional material related to the topic without leaving the chapter.

# INTRODUCTION

## WHO OR WHAT CREATED THE UNIVERSE?

Humanity has been obsessed finding the answer to the question "How, what, or who created the Universe and everything in that Universe?" From the first appearance of humanity on earth through the present time, humans have been searching for an understanding of the creation of the universe and their relationship to the universe. Our understanding of what or who created humanity and the universe has changed over the centuries. [From **HIDDEN HEART OF THE COSMOS - Humanity and New Story**. by Heyward Brian Thomas Swimme (2019).]

The most recent cosmology is that the modern world, which has produced the narrative that stars with the Big Bang and marched forward from the simplest beginning to the complex world today. Elementary particles join together to form nuclei of various light elements such as hydrogen, helium and lithium. As the universe expanded and cooled, the first atoms were drawn together by the gravitational attraction of baryonic (ordinary) matter and dark matter into a star and Galaxy. Some of the early stars ended in a violent explosions out of which all of the heavy elements were synthesized, everything from beryllium to carbon to uranium. On the rocky planet, chemical reactions brought forth cellular life. These primary organisms gradually became involved with one another in an ongoing synthesis that led to the organic evolution of sponges, echinoderms, flowers, diverse plants and animals, including a seventy- million-year primate lineage leading to the self-reflexive consciousness of *Homo sapiens*, such as the !Kung Bushman and the Modern Human." [from **HIDDEN HEART OF THE COSMOS, Humanity and the New Story. by Brian Thomas Swimme (2019), page 85.**]

Early attempts to answer the question of the <u>pre-creation force</u> that created the Universe and everything in that Universe resulted in many different names for the <u>pre-creation force</u>: TAO, YHWH, BRAHMAN, ALLAH, AHURA MAZDA, and GOD. God is the name used in this text for the <u>pre-creation force</u>. There is only one God Who created the universe, and that God is for all of humanity.

Humanity is not capable of fully comprehending Who or what God is. Humanity has always attempted to explain, define, and describe Who or what God is. Individuals, Shaman, Prophets, Rabbis. Priest, Imam Theologians, and Religions each have their definition of God to help others to know God. The differences in the definitions can cause conflicts and confusions within and between individuals, groups, and religions. Even within a group the theology, definition, and description of who or what God is can change over time.

We need to accept the fact that humanity has a limited understanding of God and that there are many different roads to know God. Humanity has the potential to coexist with diverse groups and ideologies. How refreshing it would be if those with differing perspectives could learn to respect each other's views.

Fortunately the world around us provides unending evidence of God. Religion seeks to provide an understanding of our creator and teach us how God wants us to live. In spite of diverse beliefs affirmed by various faith communities isn't it fascinating that the Golden Rule "So in everything, do to others what you would have them do to you, for this sums up Law and the Prophets" (Mattew 7:12) is one of the corner stones of the belief system of many Religions, and clearly reveals a common bond among all who acknowledge God as creator of all.

God is the creator of the universe not part of it. Therefore, we must have faith in our limited understanding of God and live our lives by focusing on God's continuing Creation and His Revelations to us. John Shelby Spong retired Bishop of Newark states it this way: "God is rather "Being itself." God is not a noun that needs to be defined. God is a verb that needs to be lived." (In Spong, John Shelby. Unbelievable, page 60. See bibliography for reference.)

What follows is my attempt to describe and to share how my faith journey guided me to develop a most personal relationship with God. Living my life daily, focusing on my relationship with God taught me to: live in the present, approach every challenge with a Win win solution, ask the question "what would Christ want me to do", and avoid worrying about the future. All of which lead me to the conclusion that God wants everyone to live their life as Christ lived His life.

Please know this, I write not to dictate the spiritual path for all to follow, but to offer some insights from my personal journey that may provide helpful road signs and meaningful guidepost for all others in their journey.

Words from the prayer that precedes all I have written "Living the life of Christ Daily" will appear again at the beginning of each section as a means of connecting the prayers petition to the thoughts expressed therein.

# THE PRAYER

## LIVING THE LIFE OF CHRIST DAILY

Heavenly Father, we want to thank you for all the gifts you have given us, for God the Father creating us in his image and likeness, for the Son of God teaching us through Jesus to live a life of Christ, and for the Holy Spirit guiding us, protecting us and being with us all the time.

Heavenly Father, enable us to be accepting of God's love for us, as we seek to live the life of Christ reassuring that the Holy Spirit is our constant companion enabling us to accept all the challenges we meet each day in a loving peaceful way. Traveling our life with this perspective enables us to love all of God's creations.

Heavenly Father, continue to empower us to live the life of Christ daily to share Your love with everyone and to look for your love in all those around us. As you speak to us in countless ways, may we be eager to make your love real to others when we see your love in others may we be aware that is your love speaking to us.

## CHAPTER 1

# CREATION

> **God is
> the Alpha
> and the Omega.**
>
> **God created light, darkness,
> the Universe and
> everything that exists.**

**Heavenly Father, we want to thank you for all the gifts you have given us, for <u>God the Father</u> creating us in his image and likeness, for <u>God the Son</u> teaching us, through Jesus to live a life of Christ, and for the <u>Holy Spirit</u> for guiding us, protecting us and being with us all the time. God speaks to us through the Holy Spirit.**

The first book of the bible Genesis is about beginnings and tells us that God created us and everything else that exists. It shows that God is both the Creator and the Ruler of all creation. Thank You Heavenly Father for creating the Universe and everything in that Universe to be a dynamic force constantly changing from the beginning to the ending.

> "Then God said, "Let us make man in our image, after our likeness. And let them have dominion over the fish of the sea and over the birds of the heavens and over the livestock and over all the earth and over every creeping thing that creeps on the earth."
>
> So God created man in his own image, in the image of God he created him; male and female he created them. And God blessed them. And God said to them, "Be fruitful and multiply and fill the earth and subdue it, and have dominion over the fish of the sea and over the birds of the heavens and over every living thing that moves on the earth." And God said, "Behold, I have given you every plant yielding seed that is on the face of all the earth, and every tree with seed in its fruit. You shall have them for food. And to every beast of the earth and to every bird of the heavens and to everything that creeps on the earth, everything that has the breath of life, I have given every green plant for food." And it was so. And God saw everything that he had made, and behold, it was very good. And there was evening and there was morning, the sixth day." **(ESV-Genesis 1:25-31)**

## GOD'S REVELATIONS

God continues to reveal His nature and provide answers to the questions we ask. However, we often do not hear or understand the response.

## God whispers

The man whispered, "God speak to me"
and the meadowlark sang.
But the man did not hear.

So the man yelled "God speak to me!"
And the Thunder roared across the skies.
But the man did not listen.

The man looked around and said "God let me see you."
In the star shine brightly.
But the man did not notice.

And the man shouted. "God show me a miracle."
And the life was born.
But the man did not know.

So the man cried out in despair.
"Touch me God and let me know that you are here!"
Whereupon God reached down and touched the man.
But the man brushed the butterfly away and walked away.

Moral of the story: don't miss out on the blessings because it isn't packaged the way you expected. (Author unknown. Open and view this on YouTube HTTPS: // youtu.be/zf ojzPQ8l0.)

Creation provided the vehicle for God to reveal Himself. Humanity learned about God through God's revelations. Primitive civilizations developed spirituality to explain creation.

The development of spiritual beliefs by ancient people was influenced by a variety of factors, including cultural traditions, natural phenomena, and the need to explain the unknown. The earliest forms of spirituality emerged from animism. Early Irish Celtic believed that naturally occurring things such as rocks, rivers and trees had spirits. Overtime, many ancient societies developed polytheistic religions, worshiping many Gods and a monotheistic religion worshiping one God. Additional information on the development of spirituality can be found in [Appendix 1: Spiritual beliefs of Ancient People on page 22.]

American Indian tribes develop their spiritual beliefs through their relationship with nature. Each tribe: Navajo, Sioux, Apache, and Mohawk developed their own unique culture and history and spiritual traditions. Some common spiritual beliefs among American tribes include a belief in a creator or higher power, the importance of nature and the natural world, and the use of ceremonies and rituals to communicate with the spirit world. Additional information on each tribe's spiritual traditions can be found in (Appendix 2: Native American Indian Tribes Spiritual Traditions on page 24).

Ancient people and ancient tribes recognized through their relationship with nature that a supreme being existed. This awareness of a supreme being naturally led to a desire to have a more spiritual relationship with God. As the relationship to God grew their interaction with nature changed and they accepted the responsibility to respect and take care of nature. An example of their relationship with nature is: When an animal is killed for food, some American Indian tribes thank their God for creating the animal and providing the food which they appreciated. The more one appreciates God's creations in nature the more one can strengthen their personal relationship with God.

God's creation provides all of us an opportunity to learn and listen to what God is telling us. Focusing on what God has created will give us insights on how we should live and interact with our environment. God's existence is made self-evident just through observing what God the Father has created. I begin each day by walking early in the morning, occasionally pausing as I do so, to observe my surroundings – the morning skies, the rising sun, singing birds. Then I take a few deep breaths and enjoy the peace that only God can give. This uplifting experience can only happen because God created a dynamic universe and everything in it. Experiences like this are all one needs to know that God exists and wants us to have a personal relationship with Him. God continues to speak to us through the wonders of his creation.

We are exposed to God's creations (the aroma of a flower, the singing of a bird, the freshness in the air and beautiful sky) all the time. How often have we thought about why and who created something. We learn to appreciate God's creations at an early age: children love seeing butterflies, playing with small animals, and smelling a flower. Once one recognizes the existence of God then one can ask the questions why God has created something and what is God saying to us.

Try the following simple exercise which I think can help us all realize that God exists. Relax, take a moment to clear your mind of all thoughts of the past and future, and focus only on being in the present. Then close your eyes and focus on breathing by taking deep breaths, slowly inhaling through your nose and exhale through the mouth ten times. Open your eyes look around and observe everything that God created. Make a list what you saw that God created then praise the Lord for all his creations and thank the Lord for revealing Himself through His revelations. My early morning walk, described above, in which I look for God's creations concludes with a simple prayer that helps me focus on and acknowledge God's countless gifts. *"I walk with beauty before me; I walk with beauty behind me; I walk with beauty above me; I walk with beauty below me; I walk with beauty all around me; Your world is so beautiful, oh God."* (A prayer of the Navajo people in America). I try to begin each day with the peace and harmony of mind knowing God is with me.

# DEVELOPING A RELATIONSHIP WITH GOD

Once we realize and accept the existence of God then we can begin to develop a personal relationship with God which develops and strengthens over time through multiple experiences one has with all of God's creations. God created us as a temple in His image and likeness and assigned us the stewardship to take care of all His creations.

Our attempt to define God in humanity terms is truly limited because God existed before creation and God created the universe and is not in it. Our ability to define and understand God is limited to God's Divine Revelations disclosure to us. Diverse cultures developed different understandings, religions, and different names for same God based on their understand of God's Revelations to humanity.

Through creation God has communicated his expectations and his will to all of humanity. God created us in His image and likeness and assigned us the stewardship to take care of all of God's creations. Diverse cultures developed different views of who or what God is based on their understanding of God's Revelation which resulted in eight different predominant philosophies, religions, and names for God.

Our attempt to define God in human terms is truly limited because God existed before creation and God created the universe and is not in it. Our ability to define and understand God is limited to God's divine revelations to us. Through creation God has communicated his expectations and his will to all humanity God created us in his image and likeness and assigned us the stewardship to take care of all his creations once we realize and accept the existence of God then we can begin to develop a personal relationship with him which hopefully develops and strengthens over time through multiple experiences we have with all of God's creation. Diverse cultures develop different views of who or what God is based on their understanding of God's revelation. This resulted in eight different predominant philosophies, religions, and names for God.

**Buddhism** is a religion and philosophy that originated in ancient India. It is based on the teachings of the Buddha, or "enlightened one," who lived in the 5th century BCE. Buddhism spread throughout Asia and has evolved into a variety of different traditions, including Theravada and Mahayana.

**Christianity** is a monotheistic religion that is based on the life and teachings of Jesus of Nazareth, who is the central figure of the religion and is also known as the Christ or the Messiah.

**Confucianism** is a system of thought and behavior originating in ancient China, developed from the teachings of the Chinese philosopher Confucius. Confucianism has played a significant role in shaping Chinese culture, society, and politics throughout history and continues to do so today.

**Hinduism** is a major religion in India and Nepal, characterized by a belief in reincarnation and a supreme being who can take on many forms. It is considered one of the oldest religions in the world and it's estimated that it has more than 1 billion followers.

**Islam** is a monotheistic religion founded in the 7th century by the prophet Muhammad in what is now

Saudi Arabia. The largest denomination of Islam is Sunnis, while second largest is Shi'as.

**Judaism** is centered around the belief in one God and the adherence to religious laws and traditions as stated in the Torah. It is a way of life that encompasses religious observance, ethical conduct, and social justice.

**Taoism** is a philosophical and religious tradition that originated in China. The word "Tao" means "path" or "way," and the central concept of Taoism is the idea of living in harmony with the Tao.

**Zoroastrianism** is an ancient religion that originated in the eastern part of ancient Persia, emphasizes the worship of one god and the concept of free will and personal responsibility. The religion has had a significant influence on other religions, such as Judaism, Christianity, and Islam. (**Appendix 3: Eight different predominant philosophies, religions, and names for God on page18.**}

Each of the above different philosophies, religions, and names for God developed from one common cornerstone belief on how humanity should live and that cornerstone is the Golden Rule.

## THE GOLDEN RULE

**"The Golden Rule says Do to [unto] others as you would have them do to [unto] you.**
The Golden Rule – by other names, different wording, but the

same meaning – is the cornerstone of many different religions such as the following eight:

> **Buddhism:** "Hurt not others in ways that you yourself would find hurtful" (Udana - Varga 5:18).
>
> **Christianity:** "So in everything, do to others what you would have them do to you, for this sums up Law and the Prophets" (Matthew 7:12); "Do to [unto] others as you would have them do to [unto] you" (Luke 6:31).
>
> **Confucianism:** "Surely it is a maxim of loving-kindness: Do not unto others what you would not have them do unto you" (Analects 15:23)
>
> **Hinduism:** "This is the sum of duty: Do naught unto others which would cause you pain if done to you" (Mahabharata 5:1517).
>
> **Islam:** "No one of you is a believer until he desires for his brother that which he desires for himself" (Sunnah).
>
> **Judaism:** "What is hateful to you, do not to your fellowmen. This is the entire law: all the rest is commentary" (Talmud, Shabbat 31a).
>
> **Taoism:** "Regard your neighbor's gain as your own gains and your neighbor's loss as your own loss" (Tai Shang Kan Ying P'ien). I interpret that to mean the following: do not be jealous of your neighbor's gain but be happy for him; and when your neighbor suffers loss, show compassion for him. Comfort him and help him.
>
> **Zoroastrianism:** "That nature alone is good which refrains from doing unto another whatsoever is not good for itself" (Dadistan-i-dinik 94:5)."

(Copied from <u>GOLDEN RULE OR $GREEDY RULE$ High-Definition Awareness and Action Needed Now – re total Subservience.</u> by Heyward Cassidy Hawkins (2010), page 2.)

God revealed the Golden Rule to diverse cultures so all of humanity could cultivate an understanding of how to live and strengthen their relationship with God. Prayer, meditation, song, communal worship, reading scripture, and organized religion all offer opportunities for us to strengthen our personal relationship with God.

God's creation of the universe and everything in that universe provides unlimited opportunities for individuals to realize and except the existence of God. All one has to do is take the time to clear their mind of all thoughts of the past and the future; focus on being present using all your senses (sight, taste, touch, hearing, and smell) to gather information to answer the question who created the presence? Being aware of the presence and focusing on the present experience to realize the existence of God is not easy. One must first focus on what God is telling us through this experience and then respond to experience. Typically we respond to experiences and do not focus on what we could learn from the experience. God is present in everything He created.

God continued to reveal Himself after creation and before the Christian era began.

God's revelations are available throughout our life's spiritual journey and provide us many opportunities to develop and strengthening our personal relationship with God.

**Father Richard Rohr wrote, "We come to know who God is through exchanges of mutual knowing and loving. God's basic method of communicating God's self is not the "saved" individual, the rightly informed believer, or even a person with a career in ministry. God**

communicates primarily through the journey and bonding process that God initiates in community: in marriages, friendships, families, tribes, nations, schools, organizations, and churches who are seeking to participate in God's love, maybe without even consciously knowing it.

If the Trinity reveals that <u>God is relationship itself, then the goal of the spiritual journey is to discover and move toward connectedness on ever new levels</u>. The contemplative mind enjoys union on all levels. We may begin by making little connections with nature and animals, and then grow into deeper connectedness with people. Finally, we can experience full connectedness as union with God and frankly everything without connectedness and communion, we don't exist fully as our truest selves. Becoming who we really are is a matter of learning how to become more and more deeply connected." [Source Richard Rohr's Daily Meditations July 3, 2022 at cac.org]

I carry a small stone in my pocket to remind me of God's Creation during the day. Daily focusing on God's creations and His revelations develops into a peaceful knowledge of His presence. When I touch the stone, I stop what I am doing and take a moment to look around to observe God's creations and then pray the prayer of Saint Patrick:

"Christ with me. Christ before me. Christ behind me. Christ in me. Christ beneath me. Christ above me, Christ on my right, Christ on my left, Christ when I lie down, Christ when I sit down, Christ in the heart of every man who

**thinks of me, Christ in the mouth of every man
who speaks of me, Christ in the eyes that see me,
Christ in the ears that hear me."**

This creates the peace of mind knowing God is with me and I
return to what I was doing with a renewed energy.

I am a Christian who refers to God as Christ, my knowledge of
God was influenced by the fact that I was born in the United States,
of Christian parents, and brough up in Roman Catholic tradition.
The remainder of this book will describe my Christian belief and
the development my personal relationship with God which will
continue to grow every day. Hopefully, this will serve as a guide to
help others to explore and develop their own personal relationship
with their God.

# APPENDIX 1

# SPIRITUAL BELIEFS OF ANCIENT PEOPLE

(OpenAI.com is the source for the following descriptions)

The development of spiritual beliefs by ancient people was influenced by a variety of factors, including cultural traditions, natural phenomena, and the need to explain the unknown.

One of the earliest forms of spirituality emerged from <u>animism</u>, which is the belief that all objects and natural phenomena have a spiritual or consciousness. This belief was common among early human societies and was likely influenced by the close relationship ancient people had with the natural world. As they observed the world around them they attributed spiritual significance to natural objects like rocks trees and rivers. of the earliest forms of spiritual

Overtime, many ancient societies developed <u>polytheistic religions</u> in which multiple gods and goddesses were worships these gods were often associated with natural phenomena, such as the sun, moon, and stars. People believe by honoring these gods, it could control and influence the natural world.

As civilization is developed, <u>monolithic religions</u> emerged, in which one God was worshipped. These religions were often influenced by philosophy philosophical and ethical beliefs and they provided a framework for the moral behavior and social order.

In addition to these religious traditions, spiritual practices such as meditation, prayer and rituals have been used throughout history to connect with the divine and cultivate inner peace and harmony. An example a belief system that developed over time from animism, to a polytheistic religions and finally to a monolithic religions is Irish Celtic beliefs.

## EARLY CELTIC BELIEFS

Early Celtic beliefs developed into a polytheistic religion with many gods and their gods represented everything created in the universe. The beliefs of Irish Celtic included the belief that naturally occurring things such as rocks, rivers and trees had spirits. These were not necessarily good or bad spirits but could react in a certain way, depending on how they were treated. The Druids (priests) who were the mystical and spiritual leaders were the most powerful individuals in the Celtic society.

The Celtic religion believed in:

- Pleasing the Gods through worship and votive offerings.
- Afterlife where individual's immortal soul lives in another world.
- Everything (rocks, rivers, trees, plants, animals, fish, people have sp irt.

## INTRODUCTION OF CHRISTIANITY TO THE CELTIC BELIEF SYSTEM

Early Christian missionaries in the 8$^{th}$ Century introduced Christianity to Celtic in Ireland and Britain. A simplified narrative is that Saint Patrick introduced the Celtic Cross to Ireland. Some believe origins of the ring on the cross represent carry over from Celtic pre-Christian belief in Roman sun-deity Invictus. Saint Patrick used the three-leafed shamrock plant as a metaphor for the holy trinity when he was first introducing Christianity to the Celtic in Ireland.

# NATIVE AMERICAN INDIAN TRIBES SPIRITUAL TRADITIONS

(OpenAI.com is the source for the following descriptions)

**Navajo Nation** is the largest Native American tribe in the United States and has a rich spiritual tradition that has been passed down through generations. Navajo spirituality is based on the belief in a sacred and interconnected universe, where everything is connected and has a spiritual essence or life force.

At the center of Navajo spirituality is the concept of hózhó, which can be translated as "beauty, balance, and harmony." Hózhó is considered the fundamental state of being, and the goal of Navajo spiritual practice is to achieve and maintain hózhó in all aspects of life. Navajo spirituality includes a complex system of ceremonies, prayers, and rituals, which are designed to restore balance and harmony in the world.

The Navajo also believe in several deities or spiritual beings, including the Holy People, who are associated with different aspects of the natural world. These deities are believed to have the power to influence events in the physical world and are honored through ceremonies and offerings.

Central to Navajo spiritual practice is the relationship between the individual and the natural world. The Navajo believe that all beings, including humans, animals, plants, and rocks, have a spiritual essence or life force and must be respected and treated with reverence. The concept of hózhó is also closely tied to the idea of respect for the natural world, as the balance and harmony of the universe depend on the health and well-being of all living things.

**Sioux Tribe** The spiritual beliefs of the Sioux tribes are rooted in their connection to the natural world and their belief in Wakan Tanka, the Great Spirit or the Creator. They believe that all things in the universe are interconnected and that everything has its own spirit or wakan. They also have a strong tradition of using ceremonies and rituals, such as the Sun Dance and the Sweat Lodge, to connect with the spiritual world and to give thanks to the spirits. They believe in the Great Spirit or the Creator and that all things in the universe are interconnected and that everything has its own spirit.

**Apache tribe** The Apache tribes have a tradition of prayer. Prayer is an important aspect of Apache spiritual belief and is used to communicate with the spirits, to give thanks, and to ask for guidance and protection. They believed that individual prayers may be offered at any time to give thanks, ask for guidance, or to request help with a specific problem.

**Mohawk tribe** The Mohawk tribes have a tradition of prayer. Prayer is an important aspect of Mohawk spiritual belief and is used to communicate with the spirits, to give thanks, and to ask for guidance and protection. They also have a tradition of using songs, dance and drumming as a form of prayer. Daily prayer is also an important of life for many Mohawk people, and individual prayers may be offered at any time to give thanks, ask for guidance, or to request help with a specific problem.

# EIGHT DIFFERENT PREDOMINANT PHILOSOPHIES, RELIGIONS, AND NAMES FOR GOD.

(OpenAI.com is the source for the following descriptions)

**Buddhism** is a religion and philosophy that originated in ancient India. It is based on the teachings of the Buddha, or "enlightened one," who lived in the 5th century BCE. The central tenets of Buddhism include the Four Noble Truths, which hold that suffering is an inherent part of existence and that it can be overcome through the attainment of enlightenment, and the Eightfold Path, which outlines the steps to be taken to reach this state. Buddhism spread throughout Asia and has evolved into a variety of different traditions, including Theravada and Mahayana.

**Christianity** is a monotheistic religion that is based on the life and teachings of Jesus of Nazareth, who is the central figure of the religion and is also known as the Christ or the Messiah. Christians believe that Jesus is the Son of God and the savior of humanity, and that through his death and resurrection, he made it possible for people to have eternal life. The followers of Christianity, called Christians, believe in one God who is the creator of all things, and that Jesus is the son of God and the savior of humanity. Christianity is one of the major religions in the world, with millions of followers worldwide. The central texts of Christianity are the Bible, composed of the Old and New Testament. The main denominations of Christianity are Catholicism, Protestantism, and Eastern Orthodox.

**Confucianism** is a system of thought and behavior originating in ancient China, developed from the teachings of the Chinese philosopher Confucius. It emphasizes the importance of education, personal and governmental morality, and proper social relationships. Confucianism has been the dominant philosophy in China for much of its history and has also been influential in other parts of East Asia. It is not a religion in the traditional sense, but rather a system of ethical and moral principles. Confucianism focuses on the cultivation of virtue, the maintenance of social order, and the fulfillment of one's responsibilities within society. The main texts of Confucianism are the Analects of Confucius and the Book of Rites. Confucianism has played a significant role in shaping Chinese culture, society, and politics throughout history and continues to do so today.

**Hinduism** is a major religion in India and Nepal, characterized by a belief in reincarnation and a supreme being who can take on many forms. It has no single founder, and its sacred texts include the Vedas and the Upanishads. Hinduism encompasses a wide range of beliefs and practices, but some key concepts include karma (the law of cause and effect), dharma (moral and ethical rules), and moksha (liberation from the cycle of reincarnation). Hinduism also reveres a wide pantheon of gods and goddesses, including Brahma, Vishnu, and Shiva. It is considered one of the oldest religions in the world and it's estimated that it has more than 1 billion followers.

**Islam** is a monotheistic religion founded in the 7th century by the prophet Muhammad in what is now Saudi Arabia. Its central text is the Quran, believed by Muslims to be the word of God as revealed to Muhammad. Muslims follow the Five Pillars of Islam, which include the declaration of faith, prayer, fasting, charity, and pilgrimage to Mecca. They also follow the moral code and laws set forth in the

Quran and the Hadith (sayings and actions of Muhammad). The largest denomination of Islam is Sunni, while second largest I Shia.

**Judaism** is centered around the belief in one God and the adherence to religious laws and traditions as stated in the Torah. It is a way of life that encompasses religious observance, ethical conduct, and social justice. The Jewish people have a strong sense of community and tradition, and the practice of Judaism often includes prayer, study of religious texts, and participation in religious festivals and lifecycle events. The main branches of Judaism are Orthodox, Conser vative, Reform, and Reconstructionist.

**Taoism** is a philosophical and religious tradition that originated in China. The word "Tao" means "path" or "way," and the central concept of Taoism is the idea of living in harmony with the Tao.

**Zoroastrianism** is an ancient religion that originated in the eastern part of ancient Persia, emphasizes the worship of one god and the concept of free will and personal responsibility. The religion has had a significant influence on other religions, such as Judaism, Christianity, and Islam.

## CHAPTER 2

# THE SON OF GOD, JESUS CHRIST ARRIVED

## BECAUSE HE LIVES

God sent his son - they call Him Jesus, He came to love, heal and forgive.

He lived and died to buy our pardon; An empty grave is there to prove my savior lives. Because he lives, I can face tomorrow, because he lives, all fear is gone.

Because I know he holds the future and life is worth the living - just because he lives.

Heavenly Father, we want to thank you for all the gifts you have given us. …. for the Son of God teaching us through Jesus to live a life of Christ, ….

**Living the life of Christ daily requires us to share God's love with everyone and to look for God's love in every challenge, situation, and individual we meet.**

## JESUS'S CHILDHOOD, JESUS'S FOLLOWERS, AND THE FORMATION OF THE CHRISTIAN CHURCH

"The Bible does not provide a lot of detail about Jesus Christ's childhood. However, it is known that he was born in Bethlehem and raised in Nazareth. He was the son of Mary and Joseph, who were both Jewish. According to the Bible, Jesus was a carpenter and lived a simple life before beginning his public ministry at the age of 30." [Additional information on Jesus' followers can be found in Appendix 4, page 36]

## JESUS AS PROPHET

"Jesus was a brown-skinned Palestinian Jew who grew up in Nazareth, a town that was poor and marginalized, ruled and militarized by the Roman Empire…. Peasant societies were marked by an enormous gulf between rural peasants and urban ruling elites. They were politically oppressive, economically exploitative, and religiously legitimate. *Jesus confronts unjust systems and demonstrates in word and deed what God's love looks like:* Jesus, who was a peasant himself, saw all of these things happening to his people. He knew that he could not be a chaplain of the empire but was sent to be a prophet of God—one anointed by God and the people to do the work of love, justice, and liberation.

We see Jesus set it off in a nonviolent way during his ministry: he gives sight to Bartimaeus [Mark 10:46–52], and he stops a woman from being stoned to death for adultery by telling her accusers that anyone without sin could be the first to throw a stone (John 8:7). In Jesus's final week before being crucified (during the Passover, which celebrates the Jewish people's defeat of slavery), Jesus goes into the temple. There he sets it off by flipping the tables of the money changers and declaring that God's house is a place of prayer and not a den of thieves [Mark 11:15–17]" [Richard Rohr's Daily Meditation From the Center for Action and Contemplation, Week Four: Jesus as Prophet, 1-25-23.]

## JESUS CHRIST'S FOLLOWERS

"Before the formation of the Christian church, followers of Jesus Christ were known as Jews who believed that Jesus was the Messiah. They were also called "Nazarenes" or "the Way" because they believed that Jesus' teachings were the way to salvation. These followers would gather in synagogues to listen to the teachings of the apostles and other leaders who had known Jesus. They would also gather in small groups in homes for fellowship and to celebrate the Jewish Sabbath and festivals. They would also celebrate the Lord's Supper in memory of Jesus. As the number of followers of Jesus grew, they began to be persecuted by the Jewish religious leaders and the Roman authorities. [Additional information on Jesus' followers can be found in Appendix 4, page 36]

## THE CHRISTIAN CHURCH

The formation of the Christian church is believed to have occurred after the death and resurrection of Jesus, when his followers received the Holy Spirit at the feast of Pentecost. This event is described in the book of Acts in the New Testament. After this, the followers of Jesus began to be called Christians, and the Christian church began to take shape as a distinct religious community." [Additional information on Jesus' vision for the Church can be found in Appendix 5. Page 37]

## JESUS CHRIST'S TEACHINGS

Jesus Christ's teaching are the cornerstone of Christianity and have been studied and followed by countless people for over two thousands years. Jesus used parables to teach basic truths and to illustrate moral or spiritual lessons. These teachings are found throughout the Gospels and continue to inspire and guide Christians today. Some of the most important teaching focused on faith, forgiveness, compassion, repentance, service, humility, and love. Jesus emphasized the importance of <u>faith</u>, teaching that those who believe in Him will have eternal life. Jesus emphasized the importance of <u>forgiveness</u>, teaching that we should forgive those who wrong us and pray for our enemies. Jesus demonstrated <u>compassion</u> for those who were suffering and taught that we should do the same. Jesus called people to <u>repent</u> of their sins and turn to God for forgiveness and salvation. Jesus taught that we should be humble and not seek to exalt ourselves over others. Jesus taught us to <u>love</u> God and our neighbor.

Jesus Christ shows us how we should live the life of Christ and condensed all of God's commandments into two commandments: He (**Jesus**) said to him, **"You shall love the Lord your God with all your heart, and with all your soul, and with all your mind. ' This is the greatest and first commandment. And a second is like it: 'You shall love your neighbor as yourself.' On these two commandments hang all the law and the prophets."** [Matt 22:37-40, NRSV]

Developing daily plan to forester a "oneness" with Christ should include Bible Study, Meditation, and prayer. Jesus told us how to develop a personal relationship with God and all one has to do is implement the plan.

## BIBLE STUDY

Reading and studying the Bible on a regular basis strengthens our understanding of and our relationship to God. Attending a Bible class and scheduling a daily time to use the Bible is a practice that may be included in persistent prayer plan. Using the Bible in conjunction with daily devotions allows one to enhance the devotional readings.

## PRAYER

**Formal prayers** are prayers that have been written down, taught, universally accepted, and often used during worship services. A formal prayer that I frequently use is *The Lord's Prayer.*

**Morning prayers** are critical for setting the tone for the day. Morning prayers may include a prayer of thanks and praise, request for support and guidance for the day. I begin each day with a morning prayer and the reading that day's daily devotion. Here is one sample of a morning prayer.

> **"Almighty God, Father of our Lord Jesus Christ, I give you thanks for the gifts I possess and the gifts I receive from you each day. I pray that You will aid me in the identification and understanding of both my strengths and my weaknesses; Almighty God, remind me that it is not about me and guide me each day to use my gifts to fulfill Your will. Lord, give me strength to approach each challenge in a grounded way using my gifts to support Your will."** [Elliott, Richard. Reflection on Life: The journey that Influenced me to become the person I am today. Page 35]

**Mealtime prayers** Begin each meal with a prayer of thanksgiving. One needs to be thankful for both the meal and all the gifts God has given us. We need to recognize and be thankful for those we share the meal with.

**Payers before important events or meetings** Asking God for guidance and support will reduce stress, encourage collaboration, and support successful results.

**Evening Prayers** End each day with a time to meditate on the day's activities, thanking God for all that day's successes. The evening prayer should include asking Almighty God, Father of our Lord Jesus Christ for guidance and directions because He knows the way.

Practicing **a persistent prayer** plan will support one living their life to fulfill God's will and will enable one to approach each day with a feeling of inner peace, a knowledge that God is always with us, and to use a win/win approach to each new challenge.

## MEDITATION

Meditation is defined as continuous and profound contemplation of musing on a subject or series of subjects of a deep or abstruse nature. Religious meditation is contemplation of spiritual matters (on religious or philosophical subjects). Meditation is a useful tool for thoughtful reflection on God's will and developing your personal relationship to God. Scheduling a time for daily meditation will strengthen one's understanding of God's will and accepting that the Holy Spirit exists within each of us and enables us to accept God's love and approach life with a win-win attitude while rejecting a win loose attitude of dualistic thinking.

Jesus speaks to the role of the Holy Spirit in us. "I have said these things to you while I am still with you. But the Advocate, the

Holy Spirit, whom the Father will send in my name, will teach you everything, and remind you of all that I have said to you. Peace, I leave with you; my peace I give to you. I do not give to you as the world gives. Do not let your hearts be troubled, and do not let them be afraid. You heard me say to you, 'I am going away, and I am coming to you.' If you loved me, you would rejoice that I am going to the Father, because the Father is greater than I." [NRSV John 14:25-28]

Committing one's life to Christ by repentance, following Christ's teachings, studying the Bible, meditating on God's will, praying on the regular basis, and living the life of Christ will enhance one's ability to develop a personal relationship with God.

Jesus Christ did not come to create a new religion. Jesus came to reform the Jewish religion and to teach all people how to live their life by fulfilling God's will. Using the teachings of Jesus to change your life and live a more spiritual life by changing one's thinking from a dualistic (win lose) approach to a non-dualistic (win win) approach enables one to avoid criticisms by looking for solutions. Living the life of Christ and having a personal relationship with God will foster the development of a direct spiritual awareness of the Divine and bring us peace of mind knowing His presence is always with us. The spiritual core of Jesus's message is love, justice, and liberation. Pray for God's guidance daily.

One of my favorite prayers is attributed to St. Benedict from the 6th Century.

> **O gracious and holy God, Give us diligence to seek You, wisdom to perceive You, and patience to wait for You. Grant us, O God, a mind to meditate on You; eyes to behold You; ears to listen for Your word; a heart to love You; and a life to proclaim You; through the power of the Spirit of Jesus Christ our Lord. Amen.**

## Gospel of Union with God

The "gospel of union with God" is a term that refers to the Christian belief in the concept of salvation and being united with God. According to this belief, through faith in Jesus Christ, people can be reconciled with God and attain eternal life in heaven. The gospel of union with God is a central theme in Christianity and is expressed in various passages throughout the New Testament, particularly in the letters of Paul. The ultimate goal of the gospel of union with God is to bring people into a right relationship with God and to experience the love, peace, and joy that come from being in His presence. [Additional information on the Gospel of Union with God can be found in Appendix 6. Page 40]

> "This fresh approach to Christianity is centered on direct spiritual awareness of the Divine that is willing to offend traditional religious sensibilities, just like Jesus did. It is willing to pay the price, just like Jesus did.
>
> That "oneness" with God and each another is Jesus' hope for the church. It is firsthand communion with God and Christ that manifests in tangible Christian unity. This can only happen when the Church proclaims an authentic message that originates from genuine spiritual awareness.
>
> My recognition of this vision came after my departure from evangelicalism and subsequently going beyond progressive Christianity into a mystical spirituality rooted in the teachings of Jesus. It is the ancient and eternal gospel. It is a gospel of union with God." (Marshall Davis shared this in a devotional and expands on this subject in his book, EXPERIENCING GOD DIRECTLY)

Committing one's life to Christ and developing a persistent prayer plan including bible study and meditation will enhance your personal relationship with God. Jesus's teachings and the way He lived his life provides one with everything needed to live the life of Christ daily.

# JESUS CHRIST FOLLOWERS THE "WAY" & DESERT MYSTICS

## THE"WAY"

"The Way" is a term used in the Bible to refer to early Christians and their belief in Jesus Christ as the only way to salvation and eternal life. The term first appears in the Book of Acts, where it is used to describe the early Christian community in Jerusalem.

In Acts 9:2, it says that Saul of Tarsus, who later became the apostle Paul, was on his way to Damascus to arrest followers of "the Way". The term is also used in Acts 19:9, where it says that Paul taught the gospel of the kingdom of God in the synagogue at Ephesus, but when some of the Jews became obstinate and refused to believe, he withdrew from them and took the disciples with him, teaching daily in the lecture hall of Tyrannus. This continued for two years, so that all the Jews and Greeks who lived in the province of Asia heard the word of the Lord.

The term "the Way" emphasizes the belief of early Christians that following Jesus was not just a set of beliefs, but a way of life. It involves not only believing in Jesus as the Son of God, but also following his teachings and example in daily life.

## DESERT MYSTICS

These Ascetics lived in the deserts of Egypt, Syria, and Palestine from the third to the fifth centuries AD. They were known for their rigorous and austere lifestyles, dedicated to prayer, fasting, and spiritual contemplation.

Some of the most famous desert mystics include St. Antony of Egypt, St. Pachomius the Great, St. Macarius the Great, and St. Moses the Black. These individuals and others like them lived in extreme poverty, often without shelter or possessions, in order to focus their minds and hearts solely on God.

Their teachings and writings influenced the development of Christian monasticism and mysticism, and their legacy continues to inspire spiritual seekers today.

# JESUS' VISION FOR THE CHURCH

"It seems like every other month I am reading about the demise of the Christian Church in the United States. The most recent article was in *The Guardian,* entitled **Losing Their Religion: Why US Churches Are on the Decline.** They all say pretty much the same thing: the Christian Church is losing members rapidly, and the pandemic accelerated this trend.

Some Christian leaders are asking tough questions about what Christians can do to stanch the flow of members and church closures. My longtime friend, Dwight Moody, has been asking such questions regularly for the past couple of years. He has a podcast and YouTube channel called The Meetinghouse, subtitled *Conversations on Religion and American Life.*

He is very concerned about the influence of extremist forms of Christianity. He is searching for an authentic form of Christianity that will counteract this trend and revive the Church. In a recent email to me he phrased it this way: "What version of Christian faith and practice will present to the modern world (or even to the Christian community) a coherent and compelling vision for human life?"

Jesus has such a vision for the Church. My recognition of this vision came after my departure from evangelicalism and subsequently going beyond progressive Christianity into a mystical spirituality rooted in the teachings of Jesus. It is the ancient and eternal gospel. It is a gospel of union with God.

Christianity is declining because it is old and sick. It is deathly ill. It has a terminal illness. The stench of death is evident in the Church's never-ending scandals, noxious rhetoric, and the cancerous growth of Christian Nationalism. The death knell of the church rings in the anti-intellectual dogma and culture-war mentality of Pentecostals and Evangelicals.

That is why younger generations are abandoning the Church at an increasing rate. Americans – young and old - are spiritually hungry, but they are not finding spiritual nourishment in the church. When they step inside a church they find either tired traditionalism or mind-numbing fundamentalism, so they turn elsewhere.

They look to other spiritual traditions or to nonreligious philosophies. They look to meditation, mindfulness, Buddhism, and yoga. They look to humanism or atheism. Meanwhile the Church conducts business as usual as if it were the twentieth century, doubling down on outmoded forms of evangelism or gimmicky outreach programs.

There is a way back from this bleak picture of Christian stagnation. There can be a resurrection of the Church, but only if it is willing to die to be reborn. What is needed is a fresh look at the spiritual core of Jesus' message without the later centuries of tradition. A "red-letter" Christianity, a gospel based on the words – and spiritual experience- *of* Jesus rather than endless words and doctriness *about* Jesus.

This fresh approach to Christianity is centered on direct spiritual awareness of the Divine that is willing to offend traditional religious sensibilities, just like Jesus did. It is willing to pay the price, just like Jesus did.

Spiritual experience was the original attraction of the charismatic and Pentecostal movements. That is why they were successful. But that was before they sold their souls to emotionalism and anti-intellectualism. Likewise, Evangelicalism was originally founded on a personal encounter with the living Christ. Now it has devolved into a dogmatic religion with a secondhand belief in an imaginary friend.

Christianity only has a future if it lives in the present - in the presence of God that Jesus called the Kingdom of God. Jesus' message was a call to the transformation of the human being through union with the Father. We see his vision for his Church voiced in his prayer offered on the night before he died. He prayed:

> *"that they all may be one, as You, Father, are in Me, and I in You; that they also may be one in Us, that the world may believe that You sent Me. And the glory which You gave Me I have given them, that they may be one just as We are one: I in them, and You in Me; that they may be made perfect in one, and that the world may know that You have sent Me, and have loved them as You have loved Me."*

That "oneness" with God and each another is Jesus' hope for the church. It is firsthand communion with God and Christ that manifests in tangible Christian unity. This can only happen when the Church proclaims an authentic message that originates from genuine spiritual awareness.

Then God will pour out the Spirit on "all people." *"Your sons and daughters will prophesy, your young men will see visions, and your old men will dream dreams."* " (Posted Friday, February 3, 2023, by Marshall Davis. Saturday 9:59 AM)

# GOSPEL OF UNION WITH GOD

The concept of the gospel of union with God is not widely recognized within mainstream Christianity theology or doctrine. However it may refer to certain theological perspectives or spiritual teachings that emphasize the idea of intimate communion or union with God.

The "gospel of union with God" is a term that refers to the Christian belief in the concept of salvation and being united with God. According to this belief, through faith in Jesus Christ, people can be reconciled with God and attain eternal life in heaven. The gospel of union with God is a central theme in Christianity and is expressed in various passages throughout the New Testament, particularly in the letters of Paul. The ultimate goal of the gospel of union with God is to bring people into a right relationship with God and to experience the love, peace, and joy that come from being in His presence.

In general the term gospel refers to the good news of salvation through Jesus Christ as described in the New Testament of the Bible. It focuses on the belief that through faith in Jesus, one can reconcile with God and receive eternal life. The central message of the gospel revolves around the life death and resurrection of Jesus Christ and the salvation he offers.

The idea of union with God, sometimes referred to as "mystical union" or "divine union", is rooted in the mystical tradition of Christianity particularly in the writings of Christian Mystics and contemplatives. These individuals sort ar deeper, experimental relationship with God beyond intellectual understanding or religious practices.

The concept of union with God suggests that through spiritual practices, contemplation, and surrender to God's will, an individual can experience a profound connection and oneness with the divine. This union is often described as a mystical or ecstatic experience where the boundaries between the individual and God are transcended.

While the gospel of union with God is not a specific doctrine or theological framework within Christianity various Christian Mystics such as Saint John of the Cross, St. Teresa of Avila, and Minster Eckhart have written extensively about the pursuit of union with God as the ultimate goal of the Christian life.

It is important to note that the understanding and interpretation of such concepts can vary among different Christian traditions and individuals. Some may emphasize the personal and transformative nature of this union, while others may approach it with caution and focus more on the importance of orthodox doctrine and obedience to religious practices. **(Source Open AI.com)**

## CHAPTER 3

# THE HOLY SPIRIT

Heavenly Father, we want to thank you for all the gifts you have given us. …. and for the <u>Holy Spirit</u> for guiding us, protecting us and being with us all the time. God speaks to us through the Holy Spirit.

When we share God's love with others that love speaks to

others. **When we see God's love in others that is God's love speaking to us. Living life in this way and knowing that God is always with us will enable us to get through future challenges that we will face.**

## THE HOLY SPIRIT

The Holy Spirit is a central figure in Christian theology and is considered to be one of the three persons of the Trinity, along with God the Father and Jesus Christ. The Holy Spirit is believed to be the active presence of God in the world and in the lives of believers in God.

In the Bible, the Holy Spirit is described as a powerful force that brings about spiritual rebirth and enables believers to live a life that is pleasing to God. The Holy Spirit is also believed to give believers spiritual gifts, such as wisdom, knowledge, faith, healing, and prophecy.

> The Holy Spirit is also seen as a comforter, helper, and teacher, which helps the believers to understand the word of God and to apply it in their lives. The Holy Spirit is also as they grow in their faith and become more like Jesus Christ. In some Christian traditions the Holy Spirit is also associated with speaking in tongues which is the ability to speak in the language that one has not learned. **(James Finley, THE HEALING PATH: A MEMOIR AND AN INVITATION{Maryknoll, Obis Books, 2023) 66-67, 68-69.)**

In summary, the Holy Spirit is seen as a powerful presence in god that brings about spiritual transformation, and powers believers, and guides them in their faithful journey. **(Open AI.com is the source of this description of the Holy Spirit)**

The Holy Spirit within each of us allows us to embrace God's immanence and to develop a personal relationship with Christ by embracing Christ's will. I believe our human body is a temple for the Holy Spirit in each of us. I also believe Jesus was a temple for Christ's life on earth. Corinthians 6: 19 reads "Or didn't you realize that your body is the sacred place, the place of the Holy Spirit? Don't you see that you can't live however you please, squandering what God paid such a high price for? The physical part of you is not some piece of property belonging to the spiritual part of you." (Corinthians 6:19 in the Message MSG)

Too often we make a decision based on our physical part and never consider our spiritual part of ourselves which results in the decision based on the belief that our ego will guide us through all challenges we face and resolve our problems. Ego driven decisions are based on self esteem and in a society where decisions are often based on a win lose choice one may not get the results they wanted. Using a more spiritually based approach to decision making will produce a more successful outcome because it is based on the excluding a dualistic ego centered approach and centric using a win win solution we're. all parties can accept the solution.

Embracing the Holy Spirit in our daily lives will strengthen one's personal relationship with God. My definition of sin is not being in an intimate relationship with Christ and following his will. Life's journey and our personal spiritual journey give us many opportunities to work on activating our relationship with God. The following testimony, written by Anne Gile a Sunnyside village resident, is a sample of how one can work in developing a personal relationship with God.

# NON-PERISHABLE SPIRITUAL ESSENTIALS

**"Scripture:** John 12:35-36 (GNT) – Jesus answered, "The light will be among you a little longer. Continue on your way while you have the light, so the darkness will not come upon you; for the one who walks in the dark does not know where he is going. Believe in the light, believe in the light, then, while you have it, so that will be the people of the light."

**Message**: Sometimes I find myself in need of an emotional/spiritual lift. My thoughts of former days, events and loved ones who have passed, put my emotions into the dark. Choosing a scripture to put on the refrigerator door, each day, was starting the day with a prayer asking God for directions. When my spirit is feeling dark, God is with me, encouraging me, and bringing light to my life. Sometimes friends are the light, sometimes it's something I've have read, or the light might be a rainbow in the sky that has followed an afternoon rain shower. Sometimes I'm moved to be the light in someone else's darkness. Maybe a phone call or a note; maybe an invite for a couple coffee and cookie. Beings the light and showing care lightens the emotions and the spirit two-fold; like non-perishable, the light will never go bad. When we put light into someone else's day, it brings out the light, not only for them, but also for us as well.

**Prayer:** Lord, as our paths cross with friends and strangers, help us to remember that, as we walk in Your life, we are commanded to share it with those around us; then we will feel our own darkness lift and your light will glow brighter. In Christ's name we pray. Amen" [written by Ann Gile a Sunnyside Village resident]

# THE DARKNESS

All experiences during life's journey can result in a positive light event or negative dark event dependent on one's response to it. A death in the family, loss of a friend, losing a job, moving to a new location, failing at a task, medical problems, *and* breaking up of a relationship are just a few examples of experiences that could move one into a dark place in their life. Responding to the darkness and turning it into lightness is a very difficult task to accomplish alone. Seek support of others and pray to the Holy Spirits for the support and guidance that will help restore the light.

"¹**John of the Cross** (Juan de la Cruz) was a Spanish mystic, poet and Roman Catholic saint. He was a member of the Carmelite Order and is known for his writings on the spiritual practices of contemplative prayer and the dark night of the soul.

*John of the Cross encourages those experiencing this dark night to trust the silence that comes when we surrender our need to speak to God using our own words:*

This is no time for discursive meditation. Instead, the soul must surrender into peace and quietude, even if she is convinced, she is doing nothing and wasting time. She might assume that this lack of desire to think about anything is a sure sign of her laziness. But simple patience and perseverance in a state of formless prayerfulness, while doing nothing, accomplishes great things." **Silence** is a poem by John of the Cross (—**John of the Cross,** *Sayings of Light and Love,* **trans. Mirabai Starr}**

What we need most
in order to make progress
is to be silent
before this great God
with our appetite
and with our tongue,

for the language
he best hears
is silent love."

(**John of the Cross**, *Dark Night of the Soul*, trans. **Mirabai Starr (New York: Riverhead, 2002), 67, 68–69, 70. Richard Rohr Daily Meditation: May 10, 2022)**

## AVOIDING THE DARKNESS IN LIFE

It is difficult to avoid the darkness in all experiences, but there are ways to change the darkness to the light by changing one's response to the situation (darkness).

The Holy Spirit within each of us allows us to develop a personal relationship with Christ by embracing Christ's will over our own free will. Too often we believe we have the answer to solve our problems and face our challenges on our own without considering God's will. One should approach every new experience by being in the present, not allowing the environment to influence their reaction and based their response to be based on how Jesus would respond to dark situation. Remember that he is always with us and if we activate the Holy Spirit in our lives we will find the support we need to deal with the darkness.

Activating the Holy Spirit in one's life is a lifelong process which helps one to grow in the knowledge and understanding of the Holy Spirit and to develop a deeper personal relationship with God. Ways to activate the Holy Spirit in one's life:

1. Practicing through prayer and seeking a deeper relationship with God. This may involve reading and studying the Bible, attending church and participating in worship, and spending time in quiet reflection and meditation.

2.  Repentance and confession of sins is also a key element in activating the Holy Spirit, as it brings forgiveness and a renewed sense of God's presence.
3.  Another way is to open oneself to the Holy Spirit's guidance, by asking for it, listening to the inner voice and being willing to obey it. This may involve taking risks and stepping out in faith to do things that may seem difficult or impossible.

Activating the Holy Spirit, focusing on your personal relationship with God, staying in present, and using a win/win approach daily will enhance one's living the life of Christ and where one will be more God-centered which will lead to developing a process of spiritual transformation in which an individual becomes more aligned with God's will and purpose.

When I find myself experiencing darkness in my life I immediately try to close my eyes, take a few deep breaths, clear my mind of all thought, and focus on developing a oneness with God and wait for His peace to calm me.

## THE GOSPEL OF UNION WITH GOD

The "gospel of union with God" is a term that refers to the Christian belief in the concept of salvation and being united with God. According to this belief, through faith in Jesus Christ, people can be reconciled with God and attain eternal life in heaven. The gospel of union with God is a central theme in Christianity and is expressed in various passages throughout the New Testament, particularly in the letters of Paul. The ultimate goal of the gospel of union with God is to bring people into a right relationship with God and to experience the love, peace, and joy that come from being in His presence. (Appendix 6 page 40)

One's Spiritual Transformation will continue to grow throughout one's lifetime and be enhanced by living the life of Christ and includes the following practices in your daily program.

1. **Mystical spirituality** refers to a type of spiritual practice that emphasizes direct personal experience of the divine or ultimate reality, often through mystical or transcendent means. It is often characterized by a sense of union or oneness with the universe, a deep feeling of inner peace, and a focus on inner transformation and spiritual growth. Mystical spirituality can encompass many different beliefs, practices, and traditions from various cultures and religions, including mysticism, meditation, and contemplative prayer.

2. **Contemplation** is a type of spiritual practice that involves focusing one's thoughts and attention on a particular subject, usually with the aim of gaining insight, understanding, and a deeper sense of connection to the divine. It can involve reflection, meditation, prayer, or other forms of introspection, and is often used as a means of attaining inner peace, cultivating awareness, and fostering spiritual growth. Contemplation can be a central aspect of many religious and spiritual traditions, including Christianity, Buddhism, Hinduism, and others.

3. **Persistent prayer** is a form of prayer that involves repeating a specific request, petition, or affirmation over a prolonged period of time. It is often used as a means of seeking guidance, comfort, or divine intervention in a particular situation, or as a means of deepening one's connection to the divine. Persistent prayer can take many forms, such as repetitively reciting a mantra or affirmations, singing a song

or hymn, or silently repeating a prayer in one's mind. In some spiritual traditions, persistent prayer is seen as a way of demonstrating one's faith and trust in the divine, and of cultivating a deeper sense of devotion and surrender.

## ACCOMPLISHING THINGS WITH THE SUPPORT OF THE HOLY SPIRIT

Often, when individuals face a new challenge, task, or problem, they attempt to immediately resolve the issue without thinking and fail because egocentric thinking assumes they know the answer. Many failures could have been avoided if one takes the time to plan, analyze, and determine what's needed before acting. Avoiding egocentric thinking and living the life of Christ, staying in the present, knowing that the Holy Spirit is always with us, will enable us to live in peace and accomplish much by taking the time to seek assistance and advice on the appropriate solution.

Helen Keller once said, "Alone one can do so little: together we can do so much."

God created humanity and put the Holy Spirt in every individual. Knowing the Holy Spirit is in you and that you can activate it by building a personal relationship with God will bring you the blessings, support, guidance and the protection of the Holy Spirit.

## SUGGESTIONS TO AVOID EGOCENTRIC THINKING AND LIVE A LIFE OF CHRIST.

- Put away selfishness: Godliness does not call us to deny the reality of the egocentric predicament, but it does call us to put away selfishness
- Set your mind on things that are above: Set your thinking not only on what is true, but on what is above. Make heaven and all the realities of God in Christ the focus of your thinking
- Consider Jesus: Look to Jesus, the founder and perfecter of our faith. Consider him who endured from sinners such hostility
- Deny selfish inclinations: Jesus is clear that we are to deny our selfish inclinations and desires if we're to follow Him. We should always seek to serve others over our selfish desires

**(Source Open AI.com)**

By following these suggestions, one can avoid egocentric thinking and live a life of Christ, which will enable us to live in peace and accomplish much by taking the time to seek assistance and advice on the appropriate solution.

## CHAPTER 4

# PUTTING IT ALL TOGETHER

## CREATION - SUPREME BEING - HUMANITY

**Heavenly Father, continue to empower us to live the life of Christ daily, to share Your love with everyone, and to look for your love in all those around us.**

Humanity has always been obsessed with knowing what supreme force or being created the universe and everything in that universe? Man's early attempts to search the natural world to find an answer resulted in many different names for the pre-creation force. The different names for the pre-existing force are the results of tribal, cultural, location, and language differences of the groups finding the answer.

I believe a supernatural supreme being (God) created the universe and all things that are in it. The universe is defined as all existing matter and space considered as a whole. The cosmos, the universe, is believed to be at least 10 billion light years in diameter and contains a vast number of galaxies. It has been expanding since its creation in

The Big Bang about 13 billion years ago. God is the creator and ruler of the universe and source of all moral authority, the supreme being.

Ancient people recognized through their relationship with nature that a supreme being existed. This awareness of a supreme being developed into a spiritual relationship with God and they accepted the responsibility to respect and take care of nature. The more one appreciates God's creations in nature, the more one can strengthen their personal relationship with God.

## WHO CREATED THE UNIVERSE

God is the creator of the universe not part of it. Therefore, we must have faith in our limited understanding of God and live our lives by focusing on God's continuing Creating and sharing His Revelations to us. John Shelby Spong retired Bishop of Newark states it this way: "God is rather "Being itself." God is not a noun that needs to be defined. God is a verb that needs to be lived." **(In Spong, John Shelby. Unbelievable, page 60. See bibliography for reference)**

God assigned all of humanity the responsibility to take care of the earth and all living things on the earth. The first book of the Christian bible Genesis is about beginning and tells us that God created us and everything else that exists "Then God said, Let us make man in our image, after our likeness. And let them have dominion over the fish of the sea and over the birds of the heavens and over the livestock and over all the earth and over every creeping thing that creeps on the earth." **(ESV-Genesis:25)**

Diverse cultures developed different views on who or what God is based on their understanding of God's Revelations. Resulting in many different predominant philosophies, religions, and names for God. The eight largest religions are Buddhism, Christianity, Confucianism, Hinduism, Islam, Judaism, Taoism, and

Zoroastrianism. Each of the above religions have different names for God, different theologies, and different philosophies, yet all developed from one common cornerstone belief on how humanity should live and that cornerstone is the Golden Rule **"Do to [unto] others as you would have them do to [unto] you."** (Matthew 7:12 NRSV).

> Contemporary philosopher Ken Wilber is a wisdom teacher's *worldview recognizes that a Spirit exist.* "Ken Wilber summarizes seven major points of the perennial philosophy, or what he calls "timeless wisdom," in his Book entitled Grace and Grit. His seven points:
>
> 1. Spirit exists.
> 2. Spirit is found within.
> 3. Most of us don't realize this Spirit within, however, because we are living in a world of sin, separation, and duality -- that is, we are living in a[n]... illusory state.
> 4. There is a way out of this ... state ... of illusion, there is a Path to our liberation.
> 5. If we follow this path to its conclusion, the result is a Rebirth or Enlightenment, a direct experience of Spirit within, a Supreme Liberation, which
> 6. marks the end of ...[separation] and suffering, and which
> 7. issues in social acts of mercy and compassion on behalf of all sentient beings. (Appendix 9)

## CHRISTIANITY AND MY BELIEFS

My name for trinitarian Christian God is Christ. I believe that Jesus is the name given to Christ while living on earth. I believe Holy Spirit is the Spirit that God the Father put into all humanity when

He created us. "Then God said, "Let us make man in our image, after our likeness…." (ESV-Genesis 1:26)

> Jesus Christ shows us how we should live the life of Christ and He preached and taught everything one needs to know and do to live a life fulfilling God's will. (see Appendix 6 - Jesus' Preaching) Jesus "went throughout all Galilee, teaching in their synagogues and proclaiming the gospel of the kingdom and healing every disease and every affliction among the people." (ESV Matthew 4:23) At the Sermon On The Mount, Jesus said the following from the Beatitudes And he opened his mouth and taught them, saying:

1. "Blessed are the poor in spirit, for theirs is the kingdom of heaven.
2. "Blessed are those who mourn, for they shall be comforted.
3. "Blessed are the meek, for they shall inherit the earth.
4. "Blessed are those who hunger and thirst for righteousness, for they shall be satisfied.
5. "Blessed are the merciful, for they shall receive mercy.
6. "Blessed are the pure in heart, for they shall see God.
7. "Blessed are the peacemakers, for they shall be called sons of God.
8. "Blessed are those who are persecuted for righteousness' sake, for theirs is the kingdom of heaven.
9. "Blessed are you when others revile you and persecute you and utter all kinds of evil against you falsely on my account. Rejoice and be glad, for your reward is great in heaven, for so they persecuted the prophets who were before you. (Appendix 7 Jesus' Preaching Matthew 5:2-10)

Jesus preached the Golden Rule and addressed the following issues: anger, lust, divorce, oats, relationships, loving your enemy, giving to the needy, not to be anxious, and judging others. He gave us the Lord's prayer and taught us to pray. (see Appendix 6 - Jesus' Preaching) Jesus Christ shows us how we should live the life of Christ and condensed all of God's commandments into two commandments: He (Jesus) said to him, "You shall love the Lord your God with all your heart, and with all your soul, and with all your mind. ' This is the greatest and first commandment. And a second is like it: "You shall love your neighbor as yourself." On these two commandments hang all the law and the prophets." (NRSV Matt 22:37-40)

He showed us how to live, and if we are living life as he lived his, we are in the right spirit and going in the right direction to strengthen our personal relationship with God.

## THE HOLY SPIRIT

"Then the Lord God formed man from the dust of the ground and breathed into his nostrils the breath or spirit of life, and man became a living being." (AMPC Genesis 2:7) I believe the spirit of life is the Holy Spirit in all of us. Jesus spoke. to the role of the Holy spirt in us. "I have said these things to you while I am still with you. But the Advocate, the Holy Spirit, whom the Father will send in my name, will teach you everything, and remind you of all that I have said to you. Peace, I leave with you; my peace I give to you. I do not give to you as the world gives. Do not let your hearts be troubled, and do not let them be afraid. You heard me say to you, 'I am going away, and I am coming to you.' If you loved me, you would rejoice that I am going to the Father, because the Father is greater than I." (NRSV John 14:25-28)

I believe having the Holy Spirit in us now, we also have eternal salvation now. The Holy Spirit has the power to offer us guidance and protection. Living the life of Christ and trusting in the Holy Spirit's guidance and protection results in living a God driven life in a peaceful way.

I believe having the Holy Spirit in us now, we also have eternal salvation now. The Holy Spirit has the power to offer us guidance and protection. Living the life of Christ and trusting in the Holy Spirit's guidance and protection results in living a God driven life in a peaceful way.

# APPENDIX 7

# JESUS' PREACHING

## MATTHEW 4:23-29 ESV

### JESUS MINISTERS TO GREAT CROWDS

And he went throughout all Galilee, teaching in their synagogues and proclaiming the gospel of the kingdom and healing every disease and every affliction among the people. So his fame spread throughout all Syria, and they brought him all the sick, those afflicted with various diseases and pains, those oppressed by demons, those having seizures, and paralytics, and he healed them. And great crowds followed him from Galilee and the Decapolis, and from Jerusalem and Judea, and from beyond the Jordan.

## MATTHEW 5:1-28 ESV

### THE SERMON ON THE MOUNT

Seeing the crowds, he went up on the mountain, and when he sat down, his disciples came to him.

### THE BEATITUDES

And he opened his mouth and taught them, saying:
"Blessed are the poor in spirit, for theirs is the kingdom of heaven.
"Blessed are those who mourn, for they shall be comforted.
"Blessed are the meek, for they shall inherit the earth.

"Blessed are those who hunger and thirst for righteousness, for they shall be satisfied.

"Blessed are the merciful, for they shall receive mercy.

"Blessed are the pure in heart, for they shall see God.

"Blessed are the peacemakers, for they shall be called sons of God.

"Blessed are those who are persecuted for righteousness' sake, for theirs is the kingdom of heaven.

"Blessed are you when others revile you and persecute you and utter all kinds of evil against you falsely on my account. Rejoice and be glad, for your reward is great in heaven, for so they persecuted the prophets who were before you.

## SALT AND LIGHT

"You are the salt of the earth, but if salt has lost its taste, how shall its saltiness be restored? It is no longer good for anything except to be thrown out and trampled under people's feet.

"You are the light of the world. A city set on a hill cannot be hidden. Nor do people light a lamp and put it under a basket, but on a stand, and it gives light to all in the house. In the same way, let your light shine before others, so that they may see your good works and give glory to your Father who is in heaven.

## CHRIST CAME TO FULFILL THE LAW

"Do not think that I have come to abolish the Law or the Prophets; I have not come to abolish them but to fulfill them. For truly, I say to you, until heaven and earth pass away, not an iota, not a dot, will pass from the Law until all is accomplished. Therefore whoever relaxes one of the least of these commandments and teaches others to do the same will be called least in the kingdom of heaven, but whoever does them and teaches them will be called great in the kingdom of heaven. For I tell you, unless your righteousness exceeds that of the scribes and Pharisees, you will never enter the kingdom of heaven.

## ANGER

"You have heard that it was said to those of old, You shall not murder; and whoever murders will be liable to judgment.' But I say to you that everyone who is angry with his brother will be liable to judgment; whoever insults his brother will be liable to the council; and whoever says, 'You fool!' will be liable to the hell of fire. So if you are offering your gift at the altar and there remember that your brother has something against you, leave your gift there before the altar and go. First be reconciled to your brother, and then come and offer your gift. Come to terms quickly with your accuser while you are going with him to court, lest your accuser hand you over to the judge, and the judge to the guard, and you be put in prison. Truly, I say to you, you will never get out until you have paid the last penny.

## LUST

"You have heard that it was said, You shall not commit adultery.' But I say to you that everyone who looks at a woman with lustful intent has already committed adultery with her in his heart. If your right eye causes you to sin, tear it out and throw it away. For it is better that you lose one of your members than that your whole body be thrown into hell. And if your right hand causes you to sin, cut it off and throw it away. For it is better that you lose one of your members than that your whole body go into hell.

## DIVORCE

"It was also said, Whoever divorces his wife, let him give her a certificate of divorce.' But I say to you that everyone who divorces his wife, except on the ground of sexual immorality, makes her commit adultery, and whoever marries a divorced woman commits adultery.

## OATHS

"Again you have heard that it was said to those of old, You shall not swear falsely, but shall perform to the Lord what you have sworn.' But I say to you, Do not take an oath at all, either by heaven, for it is the throne of God, or by the earth, for it is his footstool, or by Jerusalem, for it is the city of the great King. And do not take an oath by your head, for you cannot make one hair white or black. Let what you say be simply 'Yes' or 'No'; anything more than this comes from evil.

## RETALIATION

"You have heard that it was said, An eye for an eye and a tooth for a tooth.' But I say to you, Do not resist the one who is evil. But if anyone slaps you on the right cheek, turn to him the other also. And if anyone would sue you and take your tunic, let him have your cloak as well. And if anyone forces you to go one mile, go with him two miles. Give to the one who begs from you, and do not refuse the one who would borrow from you.

## LOVE YOUR ENEMIES

"You have heard that it was said, You shall love your neighbor and hate your enemy.' But I say to you, Love your enemies and pray for those who persecute you, so that you may be sons of your Father who is in heaven. For he makes his sun rise on the evil and on the good, and sends rain on the just and on the unjust. For if you love those who love you, what reward do you have? Do not even the tax collectors do the same? And if you greet only your brothers, what more are you doing than others? Do not even the Gentiles do the same? You therefore must be perfect, as your heavenly Father is perfect.

# MATTHEW 6:1-23 ESV

## GIVING TO THE NEEDY

"Beware of practicing your righteousness before other people in order to be seen by them, for then you will have no reward from your Father who is in heaven.

"Thus, when you give to the needy, sound no trumpet before you, as the hypocrites do in the synagogues and in the streets, that they may be praised by others. Truly, I say to you, they have received their reward. But when you give to the needy, do not let your left hand know what your right hand is doing, so that your giving may be in secret. And your Father who sees in secret will reward you.

## THE LORD'S PRAYER

"And when you pray, you must not be like the hypocrites. For they love to stand and pray in the synagogues and at the street corners, that they may be seen by others. Truly, I say to you, they have received their reward. But when you pray, go into your room and shut the door and pray to your Father who is in secret. And your Father who sees in secret will reward you.

"And when you pray, do not heap up empty phrases as the

Gentiles do, for they think that they will be heard for their many words. Do not be like them, for your Father knows what you need before you ask him. Pray then like this:

> **"Our Father in heaven, hallowed be your name.**
> **Your kingdom come, your will be done, on earth**
> **as it is in heaven.**
> **Give us this day our daily bread, and forgive**
> **us our debts, as we also have forgiven our**
> **debtors.**
> **And lead us not into temptation, but deliver us**
> **from evil.**

For if you forgive others their trespasses, your heavenly Father will also forgive you, but if you do not forgive others their trespasses, neither will your Father forgive your trespasses.

## FASTING

"And when you fast, do not look gloomy like the hypocrites, for they disfigure their faces that their fasting may be seen by others. Truly, I say to you, they have received their reward. But when you fast, anoint your head and wash your face, that your fasting may not be seen by others but by your Father who is in secret. And your Father who sees in secret will reward you.

## LAY UP TREASURES IN HEAVEN

"Do not lay up for yourselves treasures on earth, where moth and rust destroy and where thieves break in and steal, but lay up for yourselves treasures in heaven, where neither moth nor rust destroys and where thieves do not break in and steal. For where your treasure is, there your heart will be also.

"The eye is the lamp of the body. So, if your eye is healthy, your whole body will be full of light, but if your eye is bad, your whole body will be full of darkness. If then the light in you is darkness, how great is the darkness!" "No one can serve two masters, for either he will hate the one and love the other, or he will be devoted to the one and despise the other. You cannot serve God and money.

## Do Not Be Anxious

"Therefore I tell you, do not be anxious about your life, what you will eat or what you will drink, nor about your body, what you will put on. Is not life more than food, and the body more than clothing? Look at the birds of the air: they neither sow nor reap nor gather into barns, and yet your heavenly Father feeds them. Are you not of more value than they? And which of you by being anxious can add a single hour to his span of life? And why are you anxious about clothing? Consider the lilies of the field, how they grow: they neither toil nor spin, yet I tell you, even Solomon in all his glory was not arrayed like one of these. But if God so clothes the grass of the field, which today is alive and tomorrow is thrown into the oven, will he not much more clothe you, O you of little faith? Therefore do not be anxious, saying, 'What shall we eat?' or 'What shall we drink?' or 'What shall we wear?' For the Gentiles seek after all these things, and your heavenly Father knows that you need them all. But seek first the kingdom of God and his righteousness, and all these things will be added to you.

"Therefore do not be anxious about tomorrow, for tomorrow will be anxious for itself. Sufficient for the day is its own trouble.

# MATTHEW 7:1-27ESV

## JUDGING OTHERS

"Judge not, that you be not judged. For with the judgment you pronounce you will be judged, and with the measure you use it will be measured to you. Why do you see the speck that is in your brother's eye, but do not notice the log that is in your own eye? Or how can you say to your brother, 'Let me take the speck out of your eye,' when there is the log in your own eye? You hypocrite, first take the log out of your own eye, and then you will see clearly to take the speck out of your brother's eye.

"Do not give dogs what is holy, and do not throw your pearls before pigs, lest they trample them underfoot and turn to attack you.

## ASK, AND IT WILL BE GIVEN

"Ask, and it will be given to you; seek, and you will find; knock, and it will be opened to you. For everyone who asks receives, and the one who seeks finds, and to the one who knocks it will be opened. Or which one of you, if his son asks him for bread, will give him a stone? Or if he asks for a fish, will give him a serpent? If you then, who are evil, know how to give good gifts to your children, how much more will your Father who is in heaven give good things to those who ask him!

## THE GOLDEN RULE

"So whatever you wish that others would do to you, do also to them, for this is the Law and the Prophets.

"Enter by the narrow gate. For the gate is wide and the way is easy that leads to destruction, and those who enter by it are many.

For the gate is narrow and the way is hard that leads to life, and those who find it are few.

## A TREE AND ITS FRUIT

"Beware of false prophets, who come to you in sheep's clothing but inwardly are ravenous wolves. You will recognize them by their fruits. Are grapes gathered from thornbushes, or figs from thistles? So, every healthy tree bears good fruit, but the diseased tree bears bad fruit. A healthy tree cannot bear bad fruit, nor can a diseased tree bear good fruit. Every tree that does not bear good fruit is cut down and thrown into the fire. Thus you will recognize them by their fruits.

## I NEVER KNEW YOU

"Not everyone who says to me, 'Lord, Lord,' will enter the kingdom of heaven, but the one who does the will of my Father who is in heaven. On that day many will say to me, 'Lord, Lord, did we not prophesy in your name, and cast out demons in your name, and do many mighty works in your name?' And then will I declare to them, 'I never knew you; depart from me, you workers of lawlessness.'

## BUILD YOUR HOUSE ON THE ROCK

"Everyone then who hears these words of mine and does them will be like a wise man who built his house on the rock. And the rain fell, and the floods came, and the winds blew and beat on that house, but it did not fall, because it had been founded on the rock. And everyone who hears these words of mine and does not do them will be like a foolish man who built his house on the sand. And the rain fell, and the floods came, and the winds blew and beat against that house, and it fell, and great was the fall of it."

## CHAPTER 5

# FINAL THOUGHTS

**As you speak to us in countless ways, may we be eager to make your love real to others. When we see your love in others may we be aware that is your love speaking to us.**

I believe having a personal relationship with God requires one to focus on their relationship with God daily. You must develop a plan and implement it by being in the present and doing God's will continuously. Developing your plan to forester a "oneness" with Christ should include Bible Study, Meditation, and prayer. Jesus told us how to develop a personal relationship with God and all one has to do is implement their plan.

"To be successful you need to learn to "let go" of the past and of future concerns, while living in the present. "The Center for Action and Contemplation teacher Rev. Dr. Barbara Holmes writes that our Western habits of acquisition and clinging make life's transitions more challenging: Transitions can only take place if we are willing to let go of what we have known, the worlds we have created, and our assumptions about "how things are." To let go is the precursor to being reborn. We discard the baggage of societal expectations and, like a morning glory, open to the possibilities of each new day, each new moment, even if those possibilities are shadowy and disorientating." (Appendix 7 - Letting Go of What We Have Known)

To letting go of the past and to stop worrying about the future allows one the freedom to make an unbiased decision in the present. One's Personal Relation with God continues to develop throughout one's life. I try to enhance my ability to stay focused on fulfilling God's will and strengthening my personal relationship with God by:

1. One must begin each day by letting go of the past, clear one's mind of the future, and live in the present by focusing on fulfilling God's will.
2. Sharing God' love in you with everything and everyone while looking for God's love in everything and everyone you meet.
3. Approaching life with a win/win attitude while rejecting a win/loose attitude of dualistic thinking.
4. Meditating daily as a way to strengthen my understanding of God's will and accepting that the Holy Spirit exists within each of us and enables us to accept God's love.

Our task is to find the good, the true, and the beautiful in everything—even, and most especially, in the problematic. The bad is never strong enough to counteract the good. We can most easily learn this through some form of contemplative practice. In contemplation we learn to trust our Vital Center over all the passing snags of emotions and obsessive thinking. Once we deepen contact with our strong and loving soul, which is also the Indwelling Spirit, we are no longer pulled to and fro with every passing feeling. This is the peace that Jesus gives, a peace that nothing else can give, and that no one can take from us (see John 14:27). (Richard Rohr's Daily Meditation on June 12, 3023}

Divine Incarnation took the form of an Indwelling Presence in every human soul and surely all creatures in some rudimentary way. Ironically, our human freedom gives us the ability to stop such a train and refuse to jump on board our own life. Angels, animals, trees, water, and yes, bread and wine seem to fully accept and enjoy their wondrous fate. Only we humans resist and deny our core identities. We can cause great havoc and thus must be somehow boundaried and contained. The only way we ourselves can refuse to jump onto the train of life is by any negative game of exclusion or unlove—even of ourselves. Everything belongs, including us.

(Adapted from Richard Rohr, *Essential Teachings on Love*, selected by Joelle Chase and Judy Traeger (Maryknoll, NY: Orbis Books, 2018), 225–226, 227.)

APPENDIX 8

# RICHARD ROHR'S DAILY MEDITATION MAY 4, 2023

**From the Center for Action and Contemplation**

## LETTING GO OF WHAT WE HAVE KNOWN

*CAC teacher Rev. Dr. Barbara Holmes writes that our Western habits of acquisition and clinging make life's transitions more challenging:*

Transitions can only take place if we are willing to let go of what we have known, the worlds we have created, and our assumptions about "how things are." To let go is the precursor to being reborn. We discard the baggage of societal expectations and, like a morning glory, open to the possibilities of each new day, each new moment, even if those possibilities are shadowy and disorientating.

Unfortunately, in the West, we don't let go of anything. We hold onto reputation and material goods long after they are no longer needed. We store acquired stuff in every nook and household cranny before renting a storage unit so that we can continue to hold onto our stuff. Dazed, we clutch at relationships long after they are on life support and cling to a past that no longer exists, grasping, desperate, and confused.

We say that we are letting go, but, in our society, letting go is more like a tug of war. We diligently guard our stories (true or not), our lifestyles, and our belief systems until they are ripped from our sweaty palms. And yet, letting go is a necessary part of transformation….

Letting go may be the only path toward rebirth. The truth of the matter is that we are clutching at nothing! The stripping has already begun. When the worst happens, our addictive desire for control and the futility of our desires are fully exposed. If we are wise, we open our minds, our hands, and our hearts, and let go.

However, I do not want to mislead you: Letting go has consequences. Finally, the striving is over, the effort to salvage and fix, be or do something, is over. It is as if we have been clinging to the wall of a mountain of our own making, a mountain of expectations, striving, and goals. When that mountain disappears, we plummet....

When we let go, the only constants are God's love and God's promise that we will never be left alone. We let go of our public persona and our striving and pursuits. Sometimes it takes a crisis to remind us that we are not in control. This space that I name contemplative is a place of breaking, relinquishment, and waiting. [1]

*Writer and former pastor Felicia Murrell describes the inherent uncertainty of transition:*

In the radiance of dark, there is process: the unfolding of mystery, things words cannot articulate, a threshold to freedom the mind cannot comprehend. But the body feels, the heart knows: This is liminality. The threshold of transition, from death to life, from evening to morn, from gestation to giving birth. The unknown is a part of it all. [2]

---

[1] Barbara A. Holmes, *Crisis Contemplation: Healing the Wounded Village* (Albuquerque, NM: CAC Publishing, 2021), 46–47.
[2] Felicia Murrell, "Liminality and Certitude," *Oneing* 11, no. 1, *Transitions* (Spring 2023): 19–20. Available in print and PDF download.

## CHAPTER 6

# SO WHAT'S THE BIG DEAL

Reverend Beth Miller calls our attention to: *"Wisdom from the world's religions which inspires us in our ethical and spiritual life.* This source expresses the idea that within each of the world's religions, there is something of value for all people. As Karen Armstrong said in our words of invocation, *religion has been an attempt to find meaning and value in life, despite the suffering that flesh is heir to.* .....This source also implies that beneath all the diversity and divisiveness of the world's different religions, there is a strong and abiding thread of common wisdom." **[Appendix 9: A Perennial Philosophy: 3ʳᵈ Source World Religions on page 58.]**

## SO WHAT'S THE BIG DEAL

So what's the big deal? Life issues remain the same, nothing ever really changes. We still face daily challenges that we just have to live with. We do not have the ability to change the dynamic forces that created the universe and continue creating everything in the universe today. Everything that God created has an alpha (beginning or birth) and then omega (ending or death). For example:

> ➤ We can't stop a storm, tornado, or flood; we must wait for each to end
> ➤ We can't end an illness, a heart attack, or pain; we can seek medical care.
> ➤ We can't end an alcohol or a drug addiction alone; we can seek help.
> ➤ Every day has a beginning and an ending; we cannot change that.
> ➤ Everything that God created has a life cycle.

## THE BIG DEAL

The big deal is that we can change how we react to the challenges we face. Rather than allow the challenge to control our response and feelings which often ends up with one feeling that they can't do anything about it and leaves one in a dark place with nowhere to turn. The big deal is we can ask for and seek help from our God and others.

My hope in writing this book about my spiritual journey and developing a personal relationship with God is not to suggest that my journey is a model for others to follow, but rather to offer some insights from my journey that may provide helpful road signs and meaningful guideposts for others in their journey.

I truly believe that everyone should have a personal relationship with God. I hope this inspires individuals throughout the world in all religions to develop their own personal relationship with their God.

Remember one cannot change the past or determine the future, therefore we need to live in the present. Approach life with a win/win attitude, look for God in everyone and everything. Preach coexistence and peace to all. I leave you with this prayer.

Almighty God, we are grateful for Your many blessings and trust in Your ultimate plan for us. Please shine Your light on all of us and surround all of us with Your love. Grant each of us a renewed spirit as we face life's challenges with renewed hope and strength along the way. Amen

# NVOCATION, READING I,
# READING 2, AND SERMON

A Perennial Philosophy: 3rd Source
World Religions
Unitarian Church of Baton Rouge
March 24, 2019
The Reverend Beth Miller

## INVOCATION

……….. from A History of Karen Armstrong

*Men and women started to worship gods as soon as they became recognizably human; they created religions at the same time as they created works of art. This was not simply because they wanted to propitiate powerful forces; these early faiths expressed the wonder and mystery that seem always to have been an essential component of the human experience of this beautiful yet terrifying world. Like art, religion has been an attempt to find meaning and value in life, despite the suffering that flesh is heir to. Like any other human activity, religion can be abused, but it seems to have been something we have always done.*

## READING I

**From Understanding the World's Religions by the Rev. Gary Kowalski**

others within our own heterogeneous communities. The days when North Americans could be comfortably classified according to Will Herberg's typology of Protestant, Catholic, and Jew are long gone (if such a time ever actually existed). Our next door neighbors and children's classmates The world contains a variety of scriptures, prophets, holy cities, and spiritual traditions. There are probably as many reasons to study the religions of the world as there are believers and seekers, doubters and devotees.

One reason might be to bring greater understanding to a planet dangerously divided by competing claims of faith. Religious violence and persecution have escalated to the point where the United Nations now reports that almost half of the armed conflicts raging on the earth at any moment are holy wars, leading some international experts to predict that the major threats to peace in the post-cold war era will come not from conflicts between secular states or ideologies, but from the clash of religious orthodoxies. If we are to achieve peace, it is critical to come to a deeper appreciation of people whose folkways and faith ways differ from our own.

Another reason to study world religions might be to learn to relate respectfully to are increasingly likely to be Buddhist or Muslim or Hindu, and we risk becoming parochial in outlook unless we deliberately extend our horizons to embrace the diversity that characterizes our society.

The most common motive for such a study may be more personal, however. Through an encounter with other faiths, it is to be hoped that we will find resources to live with greater wisdom and serenity. Fewer people today are willing to accept uncritically the religion of their parents and past generations. More are determined to explore the teachings and insights of other faiths. This is certainly true for most Unitarian Universalists.

## READING II

### —Martin Luther King, Jr.

*Some years ago a famous novelist died. Among his papers was found a list of suggested plots for future stories, the most prominently underscored being this one: "A widely separated family inherits a house in which they have to live together." This is the great new problem of mankind. We have inherited a large house, a great "world house" in which we have to live together—black and white, Easterner and Westerner, Gentile and Jew, Catholic and Protestant, Moslem and Hindu—a family unduly separated in ideas, culture, and interests, who, because we can never again live apart, must learn somehow to live with each other in peace.*

## SERMON

### ---Rev. Beth Miller

Today, we consider the third source in this sermon series on the six sources of our Unitarian Universalist statement of principles and sources. It calls our attention to: *Wisdom from the world's religions which inspires us in our ethical and spiritual life.* This source expresses the idea that within each of the world's religions, there is something of value for all people. As Karen Armstrong said in our words fo invocation, *religion has been an attempt to find meaning and value in life, despite the suffering that flesh is heir to.*

And while she reminds us that *religion can be abused,* it seems that trying to answer those persistent human questions about how life came to be and what it means, our search for meaning and value, is *something we have always done.*

This source also implies that beneath all the diversity and

divisiveness of the world's different religions, there is a strong and abiding thread of common wisdom.

That seems odd, doesn't it? The different world's religions seem radically different and have all too often been hostile to one another. So much of what we see through history and today in the media and in fiction that lifts up the differences, how religions have been used to wage wars and to conquer enemies, to suppress people and maintain power.

This is true. We humans have been fighting about God and the nature of existence since the beginning. And we've created religions to ensconced our different points of view and we've used our religions to misuse our considerable power to exploit one another and the richness of the earth. Old Turtle told it like it is.

But that's only part of the story, right? Old Turtle called humanity not to learn something new, but to remember. To remember the innate wisdom of <u>connection</u> that is just as much a part of human beings as the <u>competition</u> and the greed that drives it.

The prophetic individuals upon whom religions were founded, like Jesus and Mohammad and the Buddha to name only a few, didn't set out to form new religions. No. They were visionaries. They had their revelations, their callings, their spiritual experiences, their visions of a better world, and they felt compelled to share them with others. Their purpose was not to build institutions. Institution builders came along later and over time, the visionaries' teachings became distorted, sometimes through misunderstanding and miscommunication, and sometimes deliberately in order to consolidate power.

Over time, and through changing power structures, the founders' prophetic messages of hope and love became diluted and sometimes contradicted. Dogma and creeds, rituals and traditions that they could never have imagined were created, either through evolution or, too often, through imposition for dubious purposes.

And as our world became smaller, or as Martin Luther King, Jr. put it: as *we inherited a large house, a great "world house" in which we have to live together*— we began fighting over the differences. **

But if we can get beneath all the madness and mayhem that religions have been used for in the world, we see that the great spiritual pioneers and visionaries <u>all</u> looked deeply <u>within themselves</u> for answers to the timeless questions, questions all human beings ask such as:

> *What is the nature of God or Ultimate Reality?*
> *Is there "something more" beyond this life?*
> *What is our true nature as human beings?*
> *Why do we suffer?*

And they found strikingly similar answers. Catholic theologian and world religions scholar, Thomas Keating in "Speaking in Silence" wrote:

> *...if we could articulate the points of agreement among the world's religions, a transcultural revelation of the basic values of human life which the world's religions hold in common would emerge.*
>
> *If we could identify the spiritual heritage of the entire human family, however diversely each religion celebrates it,*
>
> *if this consensus could then be injected with one voice into the sociopolitical arena, the world's religions would be contributing an all important spiritual dimension to the decision making process.*

Socio-political propositions are more matters of the head. Similarly, religious doctrines and dogma and rules are matters of the head - rational propositions with arguments. This is the kind of discourse that is expected and accepted in the socio-political arena. And every religion has this kind of knowledge, too. And it is in this realm, the realm of and doctrine, that we find the contradictions in religions, and even within different branches of the same religion.

But the wisdom literature in all the world's sacred writings is written from the heart, not from the head. All wisdom literature is about things like thanks-giving, finding joy in living, harmony with others and with all beings, unity with God. Wisdom points to universal human experiences rather than to specific dogma and rituals. In all the religions, it is the wisdom literature that connects followers with gratitude, joy, praise, wonder, and delight, and brings a sense of acceptance and inner peace.

That's the heart realm. It points to souls consumed with longing, not minds stuffed with specific knowledge. Wisdom is about our deep human yearning, not our mental gymnastics to prove or disprove a proposition. And wisdom is about our deep knowing of truth beyond words, and without proof.

Obviously, we need both kinds of knowing to get through life. I'm not disparaging intellect or structure or any of that. But it is in the domain of wisdom that we find commonality with people of all faiths and inspiration in our ethical and spiritual lives. And this is what our Unitarian Universalist 3rd source points us toward: not doctrines, but _Wisdom from the world's religions..._

What, then, is this wisdom we find at the heart of the world's religions?

That there is <u>a deep oneness at the heart of all things</u>; that we are a <u>part</u> of this oneness; and that there are ways to <u>directly experience</u> this oneness and to <u>grow in harmony</u> with it. Pretty much what Old Turtle told us in this morning's lesson for all ages.

Another way to think about this is to consider the difference between the "outside" and "inside" of religion. "Outside" refers to things such as customs, myths, rules, language, organization, etc.

"Inside" refers to the inner spiritual questions, direct experiences, and enlightenment or awakening of individuals. These inner experiences generally emerge de focused study.

Spiritual practices challenge us to know ourselves deeply, and, ultimately, to experience other levels of reality. We are urged to look within ourselves - look <u>inside</u> - for answers, and not simply to follow external rules. This is at the core of Unitarian Universalism. It's the 4<sup>th</sup> of our 7 principles: we covenant to affirm and promote *a free and responsible search for truth and meaning*. Truth in this context refers to capital T truth, not truth that is proven or disproven by facts and figures. Capital T truth is the kind of Truth we know intuitively exists, but which we currently cannot prove.

Over the last 15 or so years, this kind of capital T truth has become suspect. But despite Stephen Colbert's 2005 coining of the term *truthiness* meaning: *believing something that feels true, even if it isn't supported by fact;* and despite the Oxford Dictionary's 2016 word of the year, *post-truth* which they define as '*relating to or denoting circumstances in which objective facts are less influential in shaping public opinion than appeals to emotion and personal belief,* wisdom of the world's religions, and the truth we seek in our *search for truth and meaning* is this capital T kind of Truth.

*Truthiness* and *post-truth arise* out of the political climate. And those terms can certainly be applied to some religious beliefs that clearly ignore proven facts. But at a deeper level, and in the wisdom traditions within each of the world's religions, there are some common capital T Truths.

Scholars in the philosophy of religion speak of the "perennial philosophy" an idea that goes back to Plato and Aristotle. This is not unfamiliar to us. The idea that all religions, underneath all their differences, point to some common capital T Truths has long been part of Universalism. In Unitarianism, the19<sup>th</sup> century Transcendentalists also propagated the idea of a universal metaphysical Truth. The perennial philosophy says that there is a

set of truths that can be found at the core of most religions, and yet
is beyond any particular religious tradition.

Contemporary philosopher Ken Wilber calls it the:

> *worldview that has been embraced by the vast majority
> of the world's greatest spiritual teachers, philosophers,
> thinkers, and even scientists.*
>
> *It's called 'perennial' or 'universal' because it
> shows up in virtually all cultures across the globe and
> across the ages... And wherever we find it, it has
> essentially similar features; it is an essential agreement
> the world over.* [and he adds wryly] *We moderns,
> who can hardly agree on anything, find this rather
> hard to believe.*

Ken Wilber summarizes seven major points of
the perennial philosophy, or what he calls "timeless
wisdom," in his book entitled <u>Grace and Grit.</u> His
seven points:

1. *Spirit exists.*
2. *Spirit is found within.*
3. *Most of us don't realize this Spirit within, however,
   because we are living in a world of sin, separation
   and duality -- that is, we are living in a[n]...
   illusory state.*
4. *There is a way out of this ... state ... of illusion,
   there is a Path to our liberation.*
5. *If we follow this path to its conclusion, the result is
   a Rebirth or Enlightenment, a direct experience of
   Spirit within, a Supreme Liberation, which*
6. *marks the end of ...[separation] and suffering,
   and which*

7. *issues in social acts of mercy and compassion on behalf of all sentient beings.*

We can highlight some of Wilber's precepts through quotes from the wisdom literature of sacred texts from different religions. Ive asked some folks to help me with this part. (Bring them up) We'll begin with Wilbur's first contentions that *spirit exists.* Nature, Being, the Absolute, or an actual name such as God or Allah – whatever we call it, there is an overwhelming consensus throughout the world's religions that there is an <u>ultimate reality </u>which pervades all the boundaries of the universe.

> **Christianity:** *There is one God and Father of all, who is <u>above</u> all, and <u>through</u> all, and <u>in</u> you all.*
>
> **Judaism:** *Have we not all one Father? Has not one God created us all?*
>
> **Hinduism:** *God is the one God hidden in all beings, all-pervading, the Self within all beings, watching over all worlds, dwelling in all beings, the witness, the perceiver.*
>
> **Confucianism**: *Remember even when alone that the Divine is everywhere.*
>
> **Sikhism:** *There is but one God whose name is true. God is the creator, immortal, unborn, self-existent.*

**Beth:** <u>Wilbur's second contention</u>: *spirit is found within.*

> **Christianity:** *The kingdom of God cometh not with observation: neither shall they say, 'Lo here' or 'Lo there.' For behold, the kingdom of God is <u>within</u> you.*

> **Confucianism:** *What the undeveloped aspirant seeks is outside; what the advanced aspirant seeks is <u>within him- or herself.</u>*
> **Buddhism:** *If you think the Law is outside yourself, you are embracing not the absolute Law, but some inferior teaching.*
> **Shintoism:** *Do not search in distant skies for God. <u>In your own heart</u> is the Divine found.*
> **Hinduis:** *The Divine hides - hidden in the hearts of all.*

**Beth:** The third point of agreement in the wisdom of the world's religions, according to this school of thought, is that *most of us don't realize this Spirit within, however, because we are living in a world of sin, separation and duality. ...we are living in a[n]... illusory state.*

Life, frustratingly and paradoxically, seems to be structured such that the finest and most meaningful aspects are not immediately apparent to us. They are hidden from outer exposure. The sweetness of an orange is hidden within a bitter skin. The seed of a tree, from which life will spring forth, is hidden within a hard shell.

To get beyond the duality, this false sense of separation, and to grasp the essence within, we have to look deeply and with the heart. We have to seek within oursel ves for the essence. And we can look to the guidance of whatever wisdom traditions speak to us and lead us within. Hear these wisdom quotes:

> **Hinduism:** *Deep within abides another life, not like the life of the senses, escaping sight, unchanging. This endures when all created things have passed away.*
> **Christianity:** *The peace of God, which passeth all understanding, shall keep your hearts and minds.*

**Buddhism:** *Be lamps unto yourselves. Be a refuge unto yourself. Seek not for refuge from anything but the Self. Desires and tendencies pass away. Only the Self abides.*

**Sikhism:** *Make honesty thy steed, truth thy saddle, continence thine equestrian armor, the five virtues thine arrows, and truth thy sword and shield.*

**Beth:** The rest of the precepts, fourth, fifth, sixth and seventh concepts, have to do with finding peace within ourselves, with transcending this duality or separation and knowing ourselves to be one with the divine, with God or Ultimate Reality -- and with all other beings. To repeat them:

- *There is a way out of this ... state ... of illusion,*
- *there is a Path to our liberation.*
- *If we follow this path to its conclusion, the result is a Rebirth or Enlightenment, a direct experience of Spirit within, a Supreme Liberation, which*
- *marks the end of ...[separation] and suffering...*
- *and which issues in social action of mercy and compassion on behalf of all sentient beings.*

The current Dalai Lama says:

> *each major religion of the world has similar ideas of love, the same goal of benefitting humanity through spiritual practice, and the same effect of making their followers into better human beings.*
>
> *...the great religious teachers wanted to lead people away from the paths of mis-deeds caused by ignorance and introduce them to paths of goodness.*

Though specific methods of finding the path vary - some religions say meditation, some say prayer, some alms giving, some works over faith, other faith over works, and so on ....... Though specifics vary, there are several basic concepts found in all the world's religions for getting to direct experience of Spirit -- that profound sense of oneness with all -- and bringing to an end our sense of separation and suffering. And when we are able to experience this, it naturally manifests in acts of service, mercy and compassion in our day-to-day lives.

Some of these commonly held virtues found in all the world's religions include the Golden Rule: love your neighbor, speaking truth, conquer with love, being peacemakers, forgiveness, judge not, do no harm, and be generous. Hear now what the world's religions say on such matters:

**Beth:** <u>On Loving One Another and Treating Others Kindly</u>:

> **Christianity:** *Do unto others as you would have them do unto you, for this is the law and the prophets. A new commandment I give you, that you love one another as I have loved you.*
> **Buddhism:** *Hurt not other with that which pains yourself.*
> *Full of love for all things in the world, practicing virtue in order to benefit others, this person alone is happy.*
> **Judaism:** *What is hurtful to yourself, do not to your fellow man or woman. That is the whole of the Torah, and the rest is commentary.*
> **Confucianism:** *Tzu-Kung asked: "Is there one principle upon which one's whole life may proceed?"*

*The Master replied: "Is not Reciprocity such a principle? What you do not yourself desire, do not put before others." Seek to be in harmony with all your neighbors; live in amity with your brethren.*

**Islam:** *Do unto all others as you would wish to have done unto you; and reject for others what you would reject for yourself.*

**Hinduism:** *This is the sum of all true righteousness: Treat others as thou wouldst thyself be treated.*

*Do nothing to thy neighbor, which hereafter, thou wouldst not have thy neighbor do to thee.*

**Beth:** <u>On Truth-Telling and Peacemaking</u>:

**Christianity:** *Put away lying, speak every person truth to your neighbor: for we are members of one another. Blessed are the peacemakers, for they shall be called the children of God.*

**Judaism:** *Speak ye, each one, truth to thy neighbor, execute the judgment of truth and peace in your gates. A soft answer turns away wrath, but a harsh word stirs up anger.*

*How beautiful upon the mountains are the feet of the one who brings good tidings, who publishes peace.*

**Hinduism:** *Say what is true! Do thy duty. Do not swerve from the truth.*

*With kindness conquer rage, with goodness malice, with generosity defeat all meanness, with the straight truth defeat lies and deceit. The noble minded dedicate themselves to the promotion of peace and the happiness of others - even those who injure them.*

**Buddhism:** *Conquer your foe by force, and you increase his anger. Conquer by love and you will reap no after-sorrow. When righteousness is practices to win peace, he who so walks shall so gain the victory and all fetters utterly destroy.*

**Beth:** On Judgment and Forgiveness:

**Judaism:** *The most beautiful thing a person can do is to forgive wrong.*
*Judge not thy neighbor until you are in his place.*
**Sikhism:** *Where there is forgiveness, there is God himself.*
**Buddhism:** *Judge not they neighbor. Never is hate diminished by hatred; It is only diminished by love. This is an eternal law. Hurt none by word or deed. Be consistent in well-doing.*
**Christianity:** *Then Peter came up and said to him: "Lord, how often shall my brother sin against me, and I forgive him? As many as seven times?" Jesus said to him: "I do not say to you seven times, but seventy times seven."*
*Judge not and ye shall not be judged.*
*Condemn not and ye shall not be condemned.*
*Forgive and ye shall be forgiven.*
**Islam:** *Follow that which is revealed to thee, and persevere with patience until God shall judge, for he is the best judge. Whatever good you do for others, you send it before your own soul and shall find it with God, who sees all you do.*

**Beth:** <u>On Generosity:</u>

> **Taoism:** *Extend your help without seeking reward. Give to others and do not regret or begrudge your liberality. Those who are thus are good.*
> **Judaism:** *Blessed is the one who considers the poor; the Lord will deliver him in time of trouble.*
> **Hinduism:** *Bounteous is the one who gives to the beggar who comes in want of food and feeble.*
> **Christianity:** *It is more blessed to give than to receive.*
> **Sikhism:** *In the minds of the generous contentment is produced.*
> **Islam:** *The poor, the orphan, the captive – feed them for the love of God alone, desiring no reward, not even thanks.*

Among the vital sources of Unitarian Universalism, we look to wisdom from the world's religions to inspire us in our ethical and spiritual lives; to help us find joy, love, and depth in daily life; to make us stronger human beings; and to turn our strength to the concerns of the world in acts which serve needs and move towards positive social change.

That's it. That's what *wisdom from the world's religions* is all about for inspiring Unitarian Universalists in our ethical and spiritual lives.

> **As we go forth today,**
> **may we be inspired by the Perennial**
> **Philosophy of the world's religions,**
> **May we remember who we are**
> **And may we honor the god within ourselves**
> **And within one another.**

# SELECTIVE BIBLIOGRAPHY

Davis, Marshall. EXPERIENCING GOD DIRECTLY: The Way of Christian Nonduality. Kindle e-book, 2017.

Davis, Marshall. THE TAO OF CHRIST: a Christian version of the Tao of Chin. Columbia. Kindle e-book, 2017.

Elliott, Richard. Reflections on Life: The journey that influenced me to become the person I am today. Christian Faith Publishing. 2020.

Keating, Thomas. INTIMACY WITH GOD: An introduction to Centering Prayer. New York: Cross, 2019.

Finley, James The Healing Path: A Memoir and an Invitation: Maryknoll, NY: Orbis Books. 2023.

Fox, Matthew. THE TAO OF THOMAS AQUINAS: Fierce Wisdom for hard times. iUniverse. 2020.

Loorz, Victoria. THE CHURCH OF THE WILD: How Nature Invites Us into the Sacred. MN. Broadleaf Books Minneapolis. 2021.

Lotz, Anne Graham. JESUS UN ME: Experiencing the Holy Spirit as a Constant companion. Carol Stream, IL. Tyndale House Publishers. 2015.

Rohr,. Richard. ESSENTIAL TEACHINGS ON LOVE;, selected by Joelle Chase and Judy Traeger. Maryknoll, NY: Orbis Books, 2018.

Rohr, Richard. THE UNIVERSAL CHRIST: How a forgotten reality can change everything we see, hope for, and believe. New York: CONVERGENT, 2019.

Spong, John Shelby. UNBELIEVABLE: Why Neither Ancient Creeds Nor the Reformation Can Produce a Living Faith Today. Harper One, 2018.

Swimme, Brian Thomas. HIDDEN HEART OF THE COSMOS: Humanity and the New Story Revised Edition. ORBIS BOOKS, 2919.

Taylor, Barbara Brown. HOLY ENVY: Finding God in the Faith of Other. New York: Harper One, 2019.

Wallis, Jim. CHRIST IN CRISIS: Why we need to reclaim Jesus. New York: Harper One, 1989.

Printed in the United States
by Baker & Taylor Publisher Services